The BHSII
Course
Companion

THE BHSII
COURSE
COMPANION

MAXINE CAVE

J. A. ALLEN
London

British Library Cataloguing-in-Publication Data.
A catalogue record for this book is available from the British Library.

ISBN 0–85131–712–X

© J. A. Allen & Co. Ltd., 1998

798.2307/CAV

Published in Great Britain in 1998 by
J. A. Allen & Company Limited
1 Lower Grosvenor Place
London SW1W 0EL

Typesetting and production: Bill Ireson
Illustrations: Maggie Raynor
Cover design: Nancy Lawrence
Printed in Hong Kong by Dah Hua International Printing Press Co.Ltd.

For Trebor
because he's even better than
he was before

Contents

Introduction

This book covers the syllabus of the Intermediate Teaching Test Examination, which is the second teaching qualification of the British Horse Society. It follows on from my previous book, *The Course Companion for the BHS Preliminary Teaching Test* (*PTT Course Companion* for short), in which I described the teaching of the rider from complete beginner to Novice level and showed how to plan and structure lessons.

By now a candidate ready for the British Horse Society Intermediate Teaching Test qualification should have developed good teaching technique, an ability to build a good rapport with pupils, an increased level of knowledge and understanding, improved communication skills, and a genuine enjoyment of teaching. If this book is used in conjunction with the *PTT Course Companion*, candidates will be assured that all background knowledge has been covered. For those candidates also working towards the riding section of the Stage IV examination, it will help them to put into words the qualities they are looking for when riding and schooling horses on the flat and over fences.

It is important to remember that the only way to develop teaching skills and understanding is to gain as much practical experience as possible. This includes riding a variety of horses to help you gain a feel for what your pupils are experiencing, as well as teaching as many different people as possible. Try to be self-critical. Ask yourself, do your pupils enjoy their lessons and come back for more? Can you see a real improvement in their riding and the way their horse is performing? When your pupils go to competitions are they showing improvement in their performance as the months go by?

Once a candidate has successfully taken the BHS Intermediate Teaching Test, and the BHS Stage IV examination, they become a British Horse Society Intermediate Instructor (BHSII).

Teaching and Riding Requirements for Intermediate Level

1. Both the Intermediate Teaching Test and the Stage IV examination require the candidate to have knowledge and riding ability to elementary dressage and Novice Horse Trials/Newcomers showjumping level.
2. In the teaching exam candidates must be able to teach and help riders working towards this level or already competing at this level.
3. In the Stage IV riding exam candidates must be able to ride horses schooled to this level and above, showing an ability to ride movements and transitions fluently, applying the aids correctly and smoothly, whilst maintaining a supple and balanced position both on the flat and over fences. They must also show enough "feel" and experience to be able to school and improve the horses they ride. They should be able to assess the horse's current level of training, problems it has, and for what sort of work its conformation, type, and way of going are best suited.
4. In both examinations candidates will be questioned about training and riding techniques and plans. Either from an instructor's point of view, or from the rider's point of view. Therefore, candidates need to be able to put over clear ideas and explanations, on the way the aids are applied, the purpose of using different movements, how they work horse and rider over fences, and any other aspects of schooling or competing that come into a discussion.

5. As a teacher or rider it is important to know the rules for each different area of competition. Candidates should have a current rule book for Horse Trials, Dressage, and Showjumping, and read them carefully making a note of permitted tack, heights of fences, correct clothing for the rider, grading of horses, and so on.

6. Teachers and riders should also have a dressage folder with all the current dressage tests so they are familiar with the requirements of each test.

7. In the Intermediate Teaching Test each candidate is examined on their ability to:
   a) Give a class lesson to a group of three or four riders either on the flat or using a grid of fences, lasting approximately 25 minutes;
   b) Give a lunge lesson to a rider of Stage III standard lasting approximately 25 minutes;
   c) Give a dressage lesson to one horse and rider of 35 minutes;
   d) Give a jumping lesson to one horse and rider of 35 minutes;
   e) Take part in a group discussion on equitation theory lasting approximately one hour;
   f) Give a lecturette lasting approximately 5 minutes; and
   g) Take part in a group discussion on business and yard management lasting approximately one hour.

8. In the riding section of the Stage IV examination each candidate will be examined on their ability to:
   a) Ride and talk about three different horses on the flat;
   b) Jump one horse over showjumps and a second horse over cross-country fences;
   c) Work and improve a horse on the lunge; and
   d) Take part in a group discussion on equitation theory.

1   The Class or Group Lesson

In general

a. For all group lessons the teacher should have a basic plan that he or she intends to follow that day. Plans should be flexible as horses and riders may not perform as anticipated and changes may need to be made. Whatever the plan, a basic lesson structure – as described in the *PTT Course Companion* – should be followed.

b. Group lessons can be very hard work for the teacher. There may be eight riders or more all expecting help and attention. Just keeping good control of the ride is a challenge.

c. Any good instructor will be trying to make the lesson interesting for all pupils. In trying to achieve a good level of interest some instructors fall into the trap of making exercises too complicated or demanding for the level of rider. Most riders will enjoy the lesson more if the exercises are kept simple and the teacher demands a high level of performance from each rider.

d. Make sure a group lesson does not become a series of commands which just direct the group around the school and through changes of pace. The riders want to know how to apply the aids, what aids to apply, when they have made a poor transition, how to improve the shape of the school figures, and so on. If the teacher constantly picks them up on each little point then they will be bound to show and feel improvement, and will really feel they have achieved something by the end of the lesson.

e. Make sure a group lesson never deteriorates into a private lesson for one person who is demanding more attention than all the other pupils. The whole group should feel they are receiving equal amounts of your attention. If one person is demanding more attention because they are not up to the same standard as the rest of the class, you should give them more simple exercises to do on this occasion. Speak to them after the lesson and advise them on a different group to join or suggest a series of private lessons to bring them up to standard.

The exam format

1. Throughout the exam candidates will move around the sections in pairs. For the class lesson the programme allows 50 minutes for two candidates. Each candidate teaches a group of riders for some 20–25 minutes. While one candidate is teaching, the other gives assistance, if necessary putting up jumps, moving poles, and so on.
2. At the beginning of the day each candidate will be told whether he or she is to give a group flat work lesson or a group jumping lesson.
3. If giving a group jumping lesson, the candidate is to show how he or she will build up to and work the ride over a grid of fences. There is usually plenty of time allowed for each candidate to assemble and lay out the grid before the lesson begins and helpers are provided.
4. This lesson is usually given in an indoor or outdoor school (a minimum of 20mx40m), depending on the examination centre's facilities. As the dimensions and layouts of different schools vary, each candidate will need to be prepared to assess the situation and choose the best position for their grid accordingly.
5. Each group will consist of three to four riders of Stage II to Stage III standard to whom the candidates should give an interesting, informative and stimulating lesson.

The group flat work lesson

Introduction
a. With the group lined up as a ride you should introduce yourself and then find out a little about each rider while you check that each horse's tack is safe and correctly adjusted.

b. Find out each rider's name and a little about their riding experience. For example: have they passed any exams? do they compete at a particular level? Ask if they have ridden this particular horse before and how often.

c. Keep this introduction brief, but be thorough. At this level you should be experienced enough to notice immediately if, for example, a brushing boot is coming undone or a martingale rein stop is missing.

d. Before you begin the lesson make sure that you give an explanation of what you intend to work on. You may say, "I'm going to begin today by having a look at and helping you with your work in walk, trot, and canter on both reins in preparation for jumping. Then we shall move on to jumping a grid and, hopefully, to improving the jumping technique of both you and your horse." Or, you may say, "Today I'm going to work you and your horse through the basic paces and a number of school figures and see if we can improve the way you sit and influence your horse and, therefore, the accuracy with which you ride school movements."

Content

1. The following is an example of exercises that could be used. However, you will need to be flexible as you will not know until the day you take your exam what level of horses and riders you have, what their problems may be, or what area you will be working in.

2. Throughout the lesson remember that you are teaching a group. You must keep everyone involved all the time, give individual corrections, maintain control of the group, and show that you can keep a group of riders suitably challenged so they enjoy the lesson and show improvement.

3. You may be the second candidate of your pair to teach. If this is the case, find out from your examiner whether you are to begin the lesson as if the riders have just come into the school, or whether you can continue with the group taking into account that you have seen them working for the last 20 minutes and you know they are already well worked-in.

   a. Move the ride off onto the left or right rein in closed order. Make sure they are working their horses forward in an active walk and comment on any position problems, application of the aids, or way in which the horses have begun their work. Make sure you follow through any corrections made, to a point where you see improvement.

b. Prepare the ride and send them forward to working trot. At this point you should have a feel as to whether or not they look capable of working safely in open order. To space them out have each rear file in turn make a transition to walk while the rest of the ride continues in trot. Comment on the quality of the transitions made, how the rider sat, how the aids were applied, and how the horse was working and accepting the aids.

c. With the whole ride now in walk in open order make a change of rein across the long diagonal. Comment on the accuracy of the turns, how well prepared they were, how the corners were ridden, how the riders were sitting and applying the aids. If the exercise is particularly badly ridden, then have the ride repeat the change of rein and make sure each one improves on the points that were poor.

d. Having changed the rein prepare the ride for trot and send them forward to trot. While in trot see them ride 20m circles at A and C, and/or B and E. Comment on and help them to improve the way they are applying the aids to ride a true circle. Make sure they are sitting correctly, applying the aids smoothly, and preparing the horse for turns and circles. The horses should be working in a good form. Help them to improve the way the horses are working. Change the rein once more during this exercise. Use a different turn from the long diagonal, perhaps the centre line or from E to B. Make sure the change of rein is accurately ridden.

e. With the ride going large, move them back into closed order by asking one of the riders to go forward to walk while the others trot on until they have closed up behind them. Now see each rider in canter. Lead files, in turn, ride forward to trot, establish canter, ride a 20m circle in canter then canter to the rear of the ride. With a capable group the next rider in line can begin the exercise before the other rider has finished. This keeps everything flowing and you can

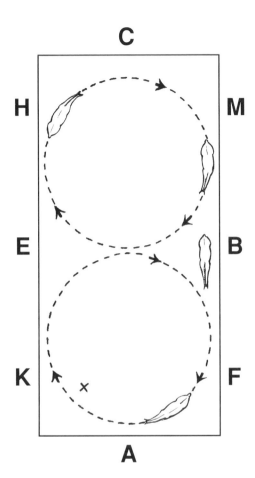

Ride in open order, riding 20m circles in trot at A and C. The instructor should be positioned at X, where he or she can see the whole ride at all times.

demonstrate your ability to keep good ride control. Comment on the rider's positions in canter, their application of the aids, the way the horse is going, and how they have ridden the transitions. Try to correct any faults you pick out and achieve improvement.

f. Move the ride back out into open order by having the lead file trot on then each of the other riders going forward to trot when there is a suitable gap in front of them. The whole ride is now in trot and they can be asked to change the rein. Again, make good use of the school

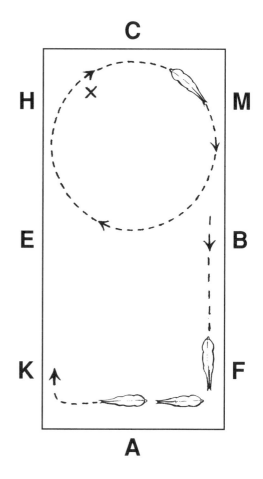

Ride in closed order while lead files in succession go forward to canter and canter a 20m circle at A or C.

and use a different school figure; perhaps a serpentine, or an inwards half-circle. Make sure the figure is accurately ridden and have the riders repeat the figure if necessary.

g. Having changed the rein, move the ride forward to walk and then halt. Look for good transitions and square halts. If not well ridden, repeat the exercise and help and correct the riders so they can achieve improved positions, application of the aids and therefore improvement in the way the horse is working for them.

Ride in open order making a change of rein using the inwards half-circle.

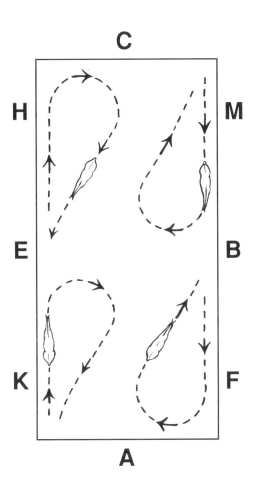

h. The ride can now work without stirrups. Make sure each rider is confident to walk, trot and canter without stirrups. The ride can walk on in open order and settle themselves in to make sure they are comfortable and have stretched their legs down a little now their stirrups are not there. Now work the ride through various school figures in walk and trot. Include transitions to halt, and some direct transitions as well as progressive. You should be helping each rider with their position, particularly through the transitions. Help them, too, with

One way of moving the ride from closed order to open order. Rear files in succession go forward to walk or halt while the rest of the ride continue in trot or walk.

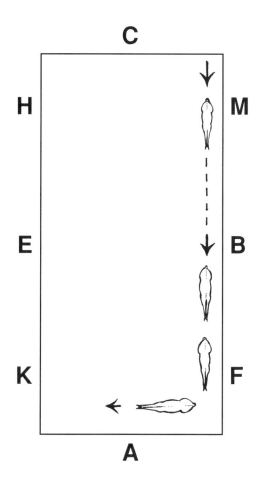

their application of the aids, accuracy of the figures ridden and with the way their horse is working. Try to show improvement in each one.

i. Providing the riders seem capable and the horses have been well behaved in their canter work, the whole ride could canter together. If the school is a little on the small side, or one or two horses are more difficult in canter, then you could have two riders walk on an inner track while the other two go large in canter. If you have a large

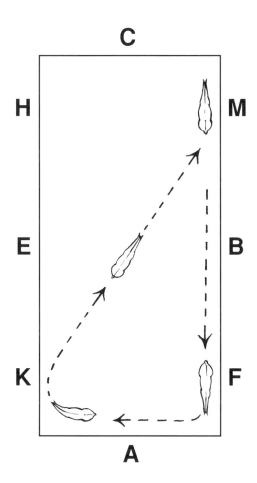

Ride in open order making a change of rein across the long diagonal.

school, you could have two riders on a large circle at one end of the school and two riders on a large circle at the other end, and all canter together. Keep helping them with their transitions, positions, and the way the horses are working.

j. After this canter work, bring the ride forward to walk and halt. Let the riders re-take their stirrups and adjust them if necessary. It will probably now be time to wind up the lesson. See the group in open order in walk and trot. If you have done the job well you should be able to show one or two transitions and school figures ridden showing improvement in how accurately they are performed, how correctly the riders are sitting and how smoothly the horses work and respond.

Conclusion

a. Line up your ride near to the examiner so that he or she can hear what you have to say.
b. Stand back from the ride so that the whole group can hear your comments, then each rider can learn a little more from the mistakes made by others.
c. Make sure each rider feels they have finished on a positive note. Tell them what you feel they have achieved and improved on as well as what you think they need more work on in the future. Never leave them feeling demoralised.
d. Ask if there are any further questions, then thank the ride.
e. Your examiner may then ask you a few questions, but not always.

The group jumping lesson

Introduction

(If you are the second candidate of the pair make sure you know whether the examiner would like you to start from scratch or continue the jumping lesson from where the previous candidate left off.)

a. This will be the same format as for the flat work lesson. Introduce yourself and find out about each rider in the same way.
b. Make sure that all the riders have adjusted their stirrups to a suitable jumping length right from the start. You only have a short time and they will need to work in at jumping length.
c. Don't forget to give an explanation of what you intend to do.

Content

a. Move the ride out onto the left or right rein in open order. Comment on and make corrections to rider's position, application of the aids, and the horse's way of going, right from the start. Send them forward to trot and see a change of rein. Continue to make corrections.

b. Progress to canter quite quickly. You could bring the ride onto an inner track and see the individual riders or two at a time go large in canter on the outer track.

c. You should have laid out jump wings and poles before beginning the lesson, so you can progress to working the ride down the line of poles you have laid out for your grid. Begin with one pole then put the others in place fairly quickly if there are no problems.

d. The most straightforward grid would be three fences with some 6.5–7m between each fence, to allow for one non-jumping stride. You will need to adjust the distances to suit the horses on the day.

e. Remember the examiner would like to assess your ability to teach a group of riders over a grid of fences. A grid only becomes a grid when there are three or more fences in the line. If you progress so slowly that you only get to jump the group over one fence you will not have shown the examiner what he or she wants to see. Therefore, you must move on through the preliminaries fairly quickly.

f. While you are at the stage of riding down the line of poles you can make frequent changes of rein, and see the riders in a forward position so you can assess their ability to remain secure and make corrections.

g. Go on to put up the first fence. A cross-pole is most inviting for horse and rider for the first jump of the session. Then, all being well, keep adding in the next fence in the line as soon as each rider has ridden the previous exercise twice.

h. You should be commenting on and correcting: the rider's approach, the quality of pace, position of the rider, the get-away, the rider's recovery, the canter lead on landing, and the way the horse is performing over the fences. There will always be something the riders can improve on. Don't fall into the trap of saying good when it isn't. However, praise should be given when it is due. This will also show the examiner that you know the difference between what is good and what is not.

i. Depending on where your grid is positioned, try to vary the approach so the riders come in from each rein. In a large school you may put the grid down the centre and be able to approach and ride away on a dif-

Distances are guidelines and need to be adjusted according to the size of horse, whether it is approached in trot or canter and whether the grid is built indoors or outside. A simple grid of three fences with a space for a canter stride between each. Fences are placed along the long side leaving the outer track free to allow riders more room to work in when not jumping.

ferent rein each time. In a smaller school the grid will probably be positioned along one side, in which case you may make the fences so they can be jumped from both sides, or alter them part way through to allow approaches from both reins.

j. If you have been the first candidate of the pair to teach this will probably bring you to the end of your lesson. If you are the second of the pair and have been asked to continue the lesson, then you may like to alter the grid a little and include a bounce followed by two fences. The two bounce fences should be approximately 3m apart, followed by 6.5m to an upright and 7m to another upright or spread fence.

k. Always check all the distances between poles and fences yourself. If a helper has put up a fence for you, just take a moment to check the dis-

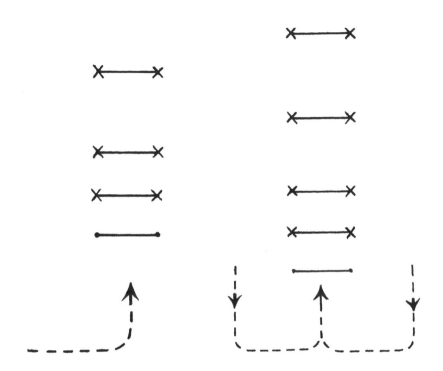

A simple grid with a placing pole followed by a "bounce" distance between the first two fences and then room for a canter stride before the last fence.

A simple grid placed along the centre line of a 30x60m arena. Using the centre line in a larger area gives more flexibility. The riders can then approach from either rein.

tance. If you have a mixed group of horses with very different stride lengths you could lay out the fences for the longer striding horses and have them approach in trot, while having the shorter striding horses approach in canter. It may be necessary to make slight adjustments to the distances for one particular horse. At this level you should demonstrate that you have the experience to make the right adjustments for the situation.

More demanding grids can be created and built at home. There would not be time to build up to a grid of this sort in the examination. Always build up to grids gradually by adding one element at a time.

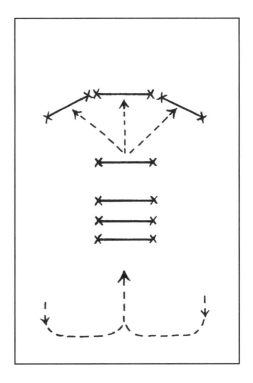

Try to keep the whole ride active. It is not helpful for horse and rider to stand still then be required to suddenly get going and jump a line of fences. The riders provided should be capable of keeping on the move and keeping out of each others way. You should remain in control of the situation and assess the right moment to give each rider a rest at halt and the right time to keep them on the move.

Conclusion

This should follow the same format as for the flat work lesson.

Common teacher faults and problems

1. Candidates often lose sight of their aims and priorities as a teacher

under exam conditions. In the flat work group lesson candidates may be seen trying to pack in as many different exercises as possible whilst completely failing to give rider help and correction. Therefore, no improvement is shown and horses and riders are being asked to perform movements for which they are poorly prepared. The quality of the teaching should be a priority. Aim to show improvement. Keep the exercises simple and make the lesson interesting by keeping the riders active, and through informative teaching.

2. For the group jumping lesson the most common mistake is not moving on to the jumping part of the lesson quickly enough. Try to strike a balance between building up progressively and being too slow. You can begin with one pole on the floor, but you only have to see the riders trot over it once before you introduce the next pole and so on.

3. Another common mistake in the jumping lesson is for the second candidate of the pair to start from scratch when the examiner has told them they can continue to progress from where the other candidate left off. You can make changes to the grid, but there is no need to completely take all the fences down and begin again with one fence. This is not progressive.

4. Don't dismiss the group lesson as an easy section that doesn't need much preparation. You must show the examiner that you can give an interesting and enjoyable lesson while maintaining good control. The group lesson, after all, is usually the bread and butter lesson of most riding schools. This is a professional exam and the examiners are looking to see that you would be employable in the profession.

Helpful hints on exam technique

a. The group flat or jump lesson is one section of the exam you can plan and practice quite well in advance. Most of us are familiar with teaching for one hour at a time, and it can be difficult to alter our way of working to a 20 minute or 25 minute lesson. Try to find groups of riders who are willing to let you practice teaching them for a 25 minute session so you can become familiar with the timing and the type of exercises that can fit neatly into this sort of session.

b. When you arrive at the centre to take the exam find out where you will be giving the group lesson and what jumps may be used. Then you can begin to make a plan of where you will build a grid or what exercises you may use in the flat lesson.

c. Try to stand near to the examiner when teaching so they do not have problems hearing you. This can be particularly relevant if you are teaching outside or near a road.

d. Make sure you are absolutely clear on what is expected of you. If you are not sure about the brief, ask the examiner again.

2 The Dressage Lesson

In general

For most instructors a great deal of their time will be spent teaching individual riders in the art of dressage. For some riders the word "dressage" conjures up pictures of horse and rider performing advanced movements that would be beyond their abilities. However, for those riders aiming to be able to ride well and communicate with their horses, all the work practised from beginner level upwards can be thought of as dressage. Teachers should have the same aims of, balance, suppleness, harmony, and lightness, for all their pupils who take riding seriously. The qualities looked for in horse and rider in all their dressage work are the fundamentals of all riding and the basis from which a rider can go on to jump show jumps or cross-country fences, go hunting, and so on.

The exam format for the dressage lesson

Each candidate is given approximately 35 minutes for the dressage lesson. A horse and rider, usually working at Elementary level or above, will be provided. Occasionally, due to illness, or lameness, horse and rider may need a last minute stand in. In this case it may only be possible to provide a combination that are working towards Elementary level, but have not yet achieved great expertise in all the required movements. The examiner will have been informed of each horse and rider's abilities, and will give a brief that takes this into account. In general the brief given will ask the candidate to improve horse and rider towards Elementary competitions.

Introduction
1. Begin in the usual way by introducing yourself and finding out your

pupil's name. Go on to quickly find out all you can about horse and rider. Ask how experienced they both are. What competitions has the horse been to? How old is the horse? Is it wearing its usual tack? Is it competing at the moment? Has the rider passed any equestrian exams? What competitions has the rider taken part in and were they with this horse? What is the rider hoping to achieve with this horse?

2. Make sure you make a quick check of the tack while you are talking to the rider.

3. Having found out a little about the combination ask the rider to show you the horse's basic paces so you can see how the pair work together. They will probably have worked-in a little already so they can be encouraged to progress quite quickly.

4. You will usually be sharing an arena with another candidate giving a dressage lesson, so make sure you keep control of your rider. Although they can use the whole arena they must not interrupt the other rider's work.

5. While the rider is showing you the horse's paces and way of going you should be watching and assessing them and be beginning to decide what you would like to work on. Although you are not really teaching them at this stage, remember your teaching time is ticking away, so keep them moving on to the next pace or change of rein when you want them to.

6. When you have had a chance to assess them ask the rider if you could have a sit on the horse to feel what it is like to ride. It is much easier to improve the horse and rider if you have ridden the horse yourself and really know what it is like. Try to quickly get a feel of the basic paces and find out how easily the horse moves away from the leg in lateral work. Try not to get carried away with schooling the horse at this stage. The aim is to find out about it so you can be of more help to the rider. You should now be ready to begin teaching the rider.

Content

1. If horse and rider are capable and the exercises will help to improve them you should try to include some work on shoulder-in and counter-

canter so the examiner can see that you are capable of teaching at this level.

2. You should have a thorough knowledge of movements required in Elementary dressage tests and should find these helpful if you base your lesson around them. In fact you may be teaching someone who is preparing for a particular test.

3. It is impossible to plan this type of lesson in advance as it will depend upon the strengths and weaknesses of the horse and rider. If the horse is a little inactive and idle you may begin with some canter work. If the horse is forward thinking and quick to respond then it may be better to begin with trot work and shoulder-in.

4. Attention to detail is important. Don't forget to help the rider with transitions and use of the school as many marks can be lost through inaccurate riding in dressage tests.

5. The rider's position may also need some correction, especially if they are adversely affecting the horse's way of going.

6. Any of the following subject matter may be included in your lesson depending upon its relevance to the horse and rider combination you have to teach.

Subject matter for lessons to elementary dressage level

At elementary level more demanding school figures and transitions are included in the dressage tests to reflect the horse and rider's higher level of achievement.

School figures and transitions

School figures include 10m circles in trot, 15m circles in canter, half-10m circles in canter, and 5m loops in counter-canter.

a. A circle of 6m, 8m, or 10m diameter may also be referred to as a "Volte". Any circles larger than 10m are referred to by the measurement of their diameter – for example, 10m or 20m circles.

b. On a circle the horse should remain "straight". This means the hind

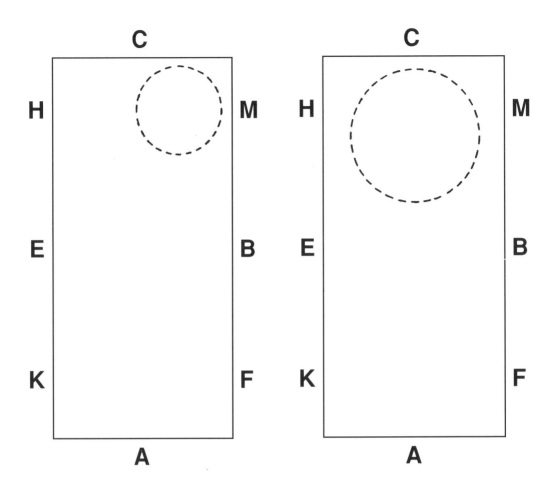

The dressage lesson (this page and opposite; reading from the left)*: a 10m circle in trot; a 15m circle in canter; a 10m half-circle in canter; a 5m loop in canter.*

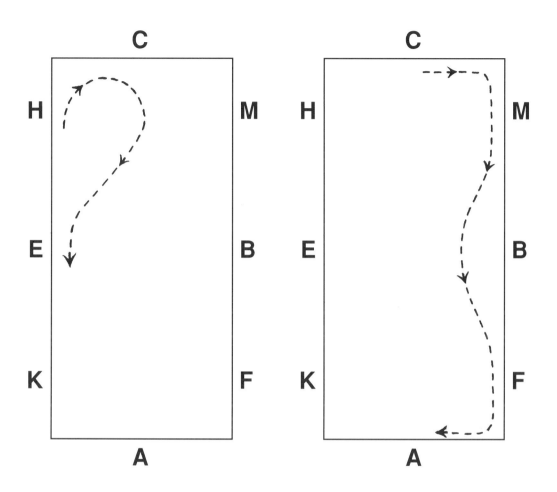

legs follow in the track of the forelegs, and the horse is uniformly bent from poll to tail along the line of the circle.

c. The horse will need to be in a more collected pace to perform these smaller and more demanding school figures accurately. The figures themselves will help the rider to improve the horse's collection.

Transitions include halt to trot, walk to canter, medium to collected trot, and medium to collected canter.

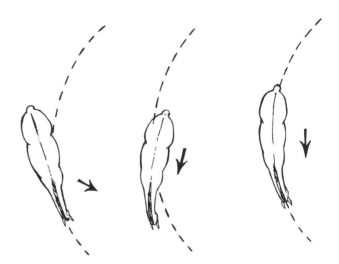

When working on a circle, the horse should be uniformly bent: (far right) *from poll to tail; the horse falling out* (centre) *through its outside shoulder; and* (near right) *the horse swinging its quarters out.*

a. Direct transitions from one pace to another, or changes of pace within the pace, should all be smooth and not abrupt.

b. When riding a transition from a medium pace to a collected pace, as in medium canter to collected trot, the rider is expected to show a little collection in the canter before making the transition to trot.

c. When transitions are required at markers, the horse should be stepping into the next pace as it passes the marker. If the transition is to be progressive, the rider will need to begin the transition just before the marker.

Terms often used

Balance

a. By asking the horse to carry a rider we upset its natural balance to a certain extent and it needs to learn how to adjust.

b. The horse's balance is further upset by unbalanced riders, or riders shifting their weight at an inappropriate time.

c. The horse needs to be encouraged to bring its hind quarters more actively under its body to support the rider, rather than letting all its weight drop on to its forehand. With too much weight on the forehand the horse becomes downhill and heavy to ride. It is difficult to manoeuvre. It becomes strong in response to the rein aids and will be inclined to rush or at the other extreme be very idle in response to leg aids.

d. When a horse is able to carry its rider keeping a good outline and smooth regular paces through turns, circles, and transitions, then it is well balanced.

e. Loss of balance in the horse shows itself when the horse is very on its forehand, hind quarters not engaged, falling in and rushing around turns and circles, falling into downwards transitions, and so on.

f. The horse will become balanced when it is able to carry an even amount of weight over its quarters and forehand, rather than having an overloaded forehand. This will be achieved through training, some horses finding it easier than others according to their type and conformation.

Horse working in a good outline

A good balanced position.

g. Balance is also vital to the rider. A well-balanced rider is sitting in a good classical position, with their ears, shoulders, hips and heels in a vertical line, and their weight evenly distributed on their two seat bones in the centre of the saddle.

h. When a rider becomes crooked, tipped forward, behind the vertical, and so on, then they are no longer in balance and will also cause the horse to lose balance.

On the forehand

a. Horses are naturally built with more weight on their forehand as the

(Opposite page) *The rider must work to achieve the correct balanced position. Here* (top) *she is out of balance, with her legs pushed forward and her seat at the back of the saddle; her seat* (centre) *is now in the deepest part of the saddle but her upper body is collapsed and her heels drawing up; now* (below) *she is in a good balanced position.*

forehand is helping to carry their head and neck.

b. When a rider is mounted, this also puts more weight on to the forehand.

c. Therefore, as already mentioned, through training we should encourage the horse to move its hind legs more underneath its body to take some of the weight and lighten the forehand.

d. If the horse is not using its hind quarters actively, but tending to push itself forward with its hind limbs rather than stepping underneath its body, it will inevitably continue to push its weight on to its forehand.

e. It is when the horse is moving in this incorrect and inactive way that it is said to be on its forehand.

Rhythm and tempo

a. Rhythm is the regularity of the footfalls in each pace, and tempo is the speed of the footfalls.

b. The rider should aim for a regular rhythm in all paces and a regular steady tempo. They should be aware of feeling for the horse's natural tempo, and make sure they don't hurry the horse and push it to a point where it loses its rhythm.

Outline

a. When the horse's hind legs are trailing behind it, and its head is held high, or its neck is outstretched with a "poking" nose, then its back is hollow and it will have difficulty in carrying the rider.

b. A horse in a good, rounded, outline is one which has its hind legs well engaged under its body. Its forehand is light and raised. Its neck is arched with a flexed poll, so its head is carried with the front of its face slightly in front of the vertical. It is free from resistance and lightly accepting the bit. As a result of this, it is able to stretch and round its back. In this outline the horse can carry the rider with ease. It will be able to perform any exercises asked of it.

Above the bit, hollow, going too deep, behind the bit

a. These terms are all used when the horse is not working in a good outline and is showing resistance in some way.

A horse going above the bit and hollow.

b. The horse is said to be above the bit when its face is well in front of the vertical and its head is held high. This usually means that it is hollow and resisting.
c. The term hollow, as already used, refers to the horse's back being dipped away from the rider making it impossible for the horse to have its hind quarters engaged. The horse's back should be rounded with strong muscles and the hind quarters brought underneath.
d. Going too deep refers to the horse dropping its head behind the vertical. Providing the horse remains free from resistance and maintains a light, elastic contact, this is not a major fault. Many horses will go too deep from time to time. It only becomes a fault if it happens continuously.

Going too deep.

e. If the horse is said to be behind the bit, which must not be confused with going too deep, it has brought its head behind the vertical and is no longer accepting the contact. The horse may have dropped the contact altogether, and need to be ridden more actively forward to re-establish the contact, or it may be getting too strong which may be caused by rider error.

Working long and low

a. For the young horse, whose muscles have not yet had time to develop,

Behind the bit and over-bent.

working with a lower head carriage makes it easier for it to arch its back and bring its hind legs forward underneath it with activity. This lower, longer outline is generally referred to as working long and low.

b. The important word to remember here is "working". The horse should be moving actively forward with impulsion, not running down hill with all its weight on its forehand.

c. Many inexperienced riders misunderstand working the horse long and low, and allow the horse to stretch down, then fail to keep a consistent contact or use their leg aids to keep activity and impulsion. Consequently, the horse becomes flat and stiff.

d. Many experienced riders use long and low work with their more advanced horses as a warm-up exercise, or a winding down exercise for the horse.

Straightness

a. A horse is said to be straight when its hind legs are following in the track of its forelegs along a straight line or curve.
b. If the horse swings its quarters to either side or drops its shoulder in or out then it is not straight.

Engagement

a. The term engagement refers to the activity of the hind quarters and hind limbs and the way in which they are being used, along with acceptance of a light and consistent elastic contact.
b. If the horse is working in a good outline for its level of training, accepting the rider's aids, and using its hind quarters actively so that it is stepping forward underneath its body, not trailing its hind limbs, then the hind limbs are said to be engaged.

Collection

a. The aim of collection is to increase the horse's ability to lower and engage its hind quarters, thereby lightening its forehand, so it is easier, more mobile, and enjoyable to ride.
b. The rider, through the use of their leg and seat aids, sends the horse forward into a softly restraining hand. The horse should bring its hind legs more underneath its body showing that it can bend its joints in an active and supple manner.
c. The horse should remain in a good outline, its head and neck raised and arched according to its stage of training.

The paces and movements

Teachers and riders should never forget to pay attention to the horse's basic paces before they begin trying to execute more advanced movements. The horse must be moving freely in a supple and balanced manner in walk, trot, and canter before transitions, school figures, counter-canter, shoulder-in, etc., can be performed to the required level.

Halt

a. In halt the horse should be attentive and motionless. Standing square with its weight evenly distributed over its four feet and with each foot of the pair in line with the other, the horse should maintain a good outline and a light contact with the rider. As soon as the rider asks, the horse should be ready to move off from the halt.

b. At Elementary level the horse may be asked to remain in halt for up to 6 seconds which is quite a long time.

c. Young horses should be taught to stand still from the start of their training, but for very short spells to begin with.

d. To ride forward to halt the rider, in a supple and balanced position, should apply their legs and seat to ride the horse forward to softly restraining hands, aiming to bring the horse's hind quarters underneath it so it halts with its weight over its quarters and keeps a light forehand. As the horse steps into halt the rider should allow with their hands without losing the contact.

Common rider/teacher faults and problems

1. The most common rider fault is to use strong rein aids to pull the horse back into halt. This will cause resistance in the horse. It may halt crookedly and not square, on its forehand, and in a hollow outline.

2. Riders may forget to practise the halt, and only halt when they finish their work or wish to adjust their tack. In this instance they often fail to pay attention to the movement, drop the contact and allow the horse to trail its hind legs, be crooked, and fidget. This instils bad habits that can be hard to overcome.

3. Teachers often allow pupils to ride into halt in a careless fashion, and should be aware of making sure they follow through the work with the rider and pay attention to detail.

4. Both teacher and rider should take care to ask for the halt in various different places in the arena to prevent horses from anticipating the movement.
5. Teachers should try to use the phrase "forward to halt" when they ask the rider to make that transition. The use of the word "forward" should help to keep the rider's mind on softly restraining rein aids and stop them from pulling back.

Walk

At Elementary level all four recognised walks are required. These are: collected, medium, extended, and free walk.

a. The collected walk has a shorter stride than the medium walk. Each step should be shorter but more elevated so that the horse flexes its joints to a greater degree. It should be a marching and active pace with regular steps.
b. In the medium walk the horse should over-track – that is, the hind feet touch the ground in front of the forefoot footprints. The horse should walk out energetically with regular steps showing freedom of movement.
c. In the extended walk the horse should retain its regularity of footfalls, and – still over-tracking – cover as much ground as possible with each step. The rider will need to allow the horse to lengthen its head and neck without losing contact.
d. The free walk, just as it sounds, is a pace in which the horse is allowed to stretch out its head and neck, and take long free steps. The rider should allow the reins to slip through their fingers and give the horse its freedom.
e. In all four walks the horse should remain in a good outline lightly accepting the bit. The outline will be shorter with the head and neck more raised and arched for the collected walk. For medium, extended, and free walk the rider will allow the head and neck to be carried in a longer outline as they allow the horse to stretch forward a little more with each pace.

f. In walk the rider must follow the natural movement of the horse's head and neck by keeping their shoulders, elbows, and wrists supple and free from tension. At the same time they should have a deep seat and a supple back so they can follow the movement of the horse's back, also without tension. The leg aids should be used lightly at the girth to maintain impulsion or to create more impulsion. When collecting the walk the rider will need to softly restrain the forward movement whilst encouraging the horse, with their leg aids, to take shorter but more elevated steps.

g. When a young horse is balanced in its basic paces, moving freely and without resistance, while keeping a good outline, the rider can begin to ask for variations within the pace. They should begin by asking just a little at a time, and should find that the horse will become more supple, balanced, and "engaged" as it progresses.

Common rider/teacher faults and problems

1. When trying to collect the horse many riders use rein aids that are too strong and forget to use their leg and seat aids sufficiently to keep forward impulsion and therefore the horse's hind quarters engaged. This leads to resistance from the horse in the form of a hollow outline, irregular steps, lack of impulsion, and so on.

2. Both riders and teachers must be careful not to spend too much time in walk as it is the pace most easily spoilt, becoming tight and restricted when not ridden well. Having said that, the free walk can be used frequently to allow the horse to stretch and rest during a training session.

3. Riders often hurry the horse in walk and push it out of its natural rhythm. The rider must take care to relax and move in a supple manner with the natural swing of the walk, encouraging free and active steps without rushing the horse so it breaks into trot.

4. Teachers must remember that the free walk is part of dressage tests, and therefore a movement which needs to be practised. Rather than just letting the rider drop the reins while the horse ambles around the arena, the teacher must make sure the rider keeps riding the horse in

the free walk, to encourage long, regular steps with the horse stretching down to relax its muscles.

Trot

Three of the recognised trots are used at Elementary level. These are: collected, working, and medium trot.

a. The collected trot has shorter steps than the other trots, but the horse should be lighter and more elevated with greater impulsion.

b. The working trot is midway between the collected and medium trots. It should be an active trot showing engagement of the hind quarters, and even steps, with the horse in balance.

c. In the medium trot the horse extends its steps a little, shows greater impulsion, lengthening its outline, but maintaining balance and regularity of footfalls.

d. In each of these three trots the horse must remain in a good, round, outline. As the horse progresses it should appear to be much rounder than when working at Novice level.

e. To ride the trot effectively the rider must have a deep seat and supple back. They must be able to sit softly without tensing against the horse's trot movement. A light and steady contact should be maintained. The rider will need to use half-halts in each of the three trots to keep the horse balanced and attentive.

f. As with the walk, when the young horse is able to keep a balanced, regular and active working trot the rider can begin to introduce variations within the pace which will improve all of their work in time.

Common rider/teacher faults and problems

1. When trying to collect the trot riders often fall into the trap of using rein aids that are too strong whilst failing to use their legs and seat to maintain impulsion. They are trying to hold the horse together rather than ride it forward and together. This will cause resistance, and the horse will lose impulsion and become hollow.

2. Teachers must not expect horse and rider to work in collected trot for more than short periods at a time to begin with. A few good steps are much better than many poor steps. The teacher should encourage the rider to ride smoothly forward into a working or medium pace once a few good steps of collected trot have been shown.

3. When riding medium trot riders often fail to keep the horse in balance between leg and hand. This results in the horse running onto its fore-hand and not extending its trot steps at all.

4. Teachers must make sure the rider has prepared the horse well for the medium trot before asking the horse for this pace. This should result in good steps. Again the pace should be kept for short stretches to begin with, so the rider learns to keep the horse in balance.

5. Riders must be able to sit to the trot in a balanced and supple manner as all the trot work is ridden sitting at this level. If the rider is stiff or lacks depth of seat this will restrict the horse.

6. Another common rider fault is dropping the contact with the horse in medium trot which results in the horse running onto its forehand.

Canter

Three of the recognised canters are used at Elementary level. These are: collected, working, and medium canter.

a. In collected canter the horse takes shorter steps than in other canters. The forehand should be light and the hind quarters very active.

b. The working canter is midway between the collected and medium canters. The horse should show balanced and regular steps with good engagement of the hind quarters.

c. In medium canter the horse begins to extend its steps a little whilst remaining in balance, keeping regular steps, and lengthening its outline a little. Again the hind quarters should be engaged and create impulsion.

d. In all three canters the horse should remain in a good round outline, and accept the bit with a light contact.

e. To ride the canter well the rider needs a well established and deep seat.

Their seat should not leave the saddle, their lower back must move with the horse in a supple manner, and their arms should be free from tension to enable them to follow the horse's movement whilst keeping a light and consistent contact. The rider should keep a little more weight in the inside seat bone to counteract any tendency for the canter work to make them slip to the outside.

f. As with walk and trot, variations within the pace can be introduced once the horse is balanced, round and active in working canter.

Common rider/teacher faults and problems

1. Riders may have similar problems to those found in the trot work. They may use rein aids that are too strong for the collected work, forgetting to use their leg and seat aids. They may rush the horse for medium work and push the horse out of balance.

2. Riders often begin to sit crookedly in canter, finding themselves slipping to the outside on turns and circles or tipping forward, making it difficult for the horse to remain balanced.

3. Teachers should not expect horse and rider to sustain collected or medium canter for more than a short period to begin with. Asking the rider to remain in collected or medium paces for too long will lead to resistance or loss of balance and spoil the paces.

4. Teachers must remember to observe riders from different angles. Standing where they can see the horse and rider from in front as well as from behind will help them to detect horse and rider crookedness.

Counter-canter

a. Counter-canter is a movement whereby the rider asks the horse for the right canter lead whilst moving around the arena in a left-handed direction or, *vice versa*, asks for the left canter lead whilst moving around the arena in a right-handed direction.

b. As the rider moves the horse into counter-canter they should keep their aids for canter with whichever leg is leading. For example, if in right canter they should keep their right leg at the girth, the left leg a little behind, their weight a little more on the right seat bone and keep the horse flexing at the poll to the right.

c. This is a suppling movement as the horse is asked to maintain its flexion at the poll in the direction of the leading leg, whilst keeping the counter-canter movement without falling in or swinging its quarters out.

d. Horse and rider build up to mastering this movement by performing gentle inclines back to the track in the form of shallow serpentine loops or half circles to change the rein, so the horse keeps a few steps of counter-canter along a straight line to begin with. When the horse is more balanced and supple it will eventually be able to canter a complete circle in counter-canter.

e. For horses that have become crooked in true canter, having a tendency to swing their quarters in whilst hugging the boards with their shoulders, counter-canter is a helpful way of improving their straightness. In counter-canter the horse cannot hug the boards with its shoulders and will straighten up in order to keep its balance.

f. The counter-canter should only be introduced once the horse is balanced and in self-carriage in true canter.

Common rider/teacher faults and problems

1. Riders often lose balance and allow their weight to move in the saddle as they ride the counter-canter. This shift of weight causes the horse to lose balance so it changes leg, becomes disunited, or breaks into trot.

2. If the rider is learning the movement at the same time as the horse is learning, they may be inconsistent with their aids, fail to prepare for the movement, or follow a poor ground plan. This will lead to the horse being confused and the same problems as above.

3. Teachers must be aware of the horse and rider's level of training and understanding, and not ask too demanding an exercise to begin with. They should try to teach riders new movements on schoolmaster horses. If this is not possible they could ride the horse through the

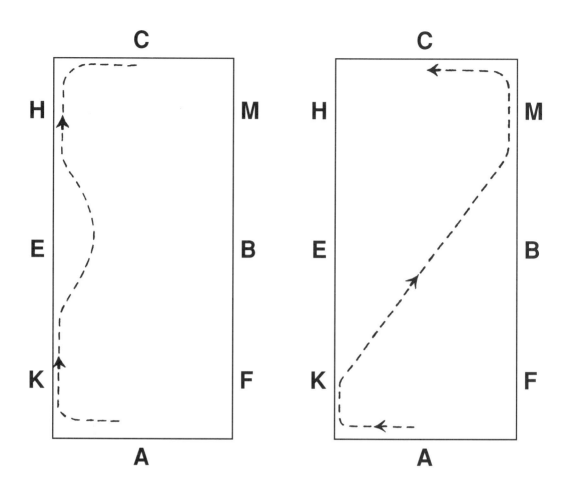

To introduce the horse to counter-canter: begin with (left) *riding a shallow serpentine; then* (right) *progress to riding canter across the long diagonal of the arena. At first, trot at* X, *then keep the canter to the track, and then for one or two strides along the track.* (Opposite page, left) *a half-circle. At first, keep the canter to the track, then trot. Then keep the canter along the track and trot before the corner. Then keep the canter around the corner. Eventually* (opposite page, right), *the horse should be able to canter a figure-of-eight without change of leg, so one half is in true canter and one half is in counter-canter.*

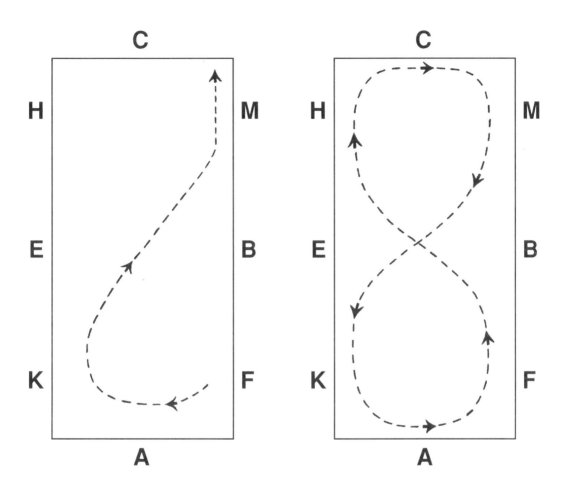

movement themselves so they give the rider a demonstration and help to teach the movement to the horse.

Simple change

a. The simple change is ridden in canter. The rider makes a change of canter lead by riding the horse from canter to walk and then directly from walk to canter on the opposite leading leg.

b. Direct downwards transition from canter to walk requires great balance, suppleness, and engagement of the hind quarters. As this transition is difficult to perform, at Elementary level the downwards transition can be progressive with two or three steps of trot before the walk. The upwards transition must be direct from walk to canter.

c. To ride the simple change the rider must take care to prepare the horse in good time for the first transition. As the downwards transition is being made the rider should be straightening the horse then changing the bend ready to strike off on the other leg. To do this they should be smoothly changing their aids. For example: if cantering with the right leg leading the rider's right leg will be at the girth maintaining impulsion. Their left leg would have been used behind the girth for the strike off, then used by the girth to help with forward activity. The right rein will have been guiding and keeping a little right flexion, while the left rein will have been controlling the speed and bend. Through a series of half-halts the rider prepares the horse and then asks for the downwards transition through trot to walk. For a moment both legs are at the girth and both reins have an equal effect as the horse is straightened from the right bend. The rider then smoothly applies the left leg at the girth and slides the right leg back behind the girth, while asking for a little left flexion with the left rein and controlling the speed and bend with the right rein. The horse is then asked to strike off into left canter directly from walk to complete the simple change.

d. The movement is particularly useful in the showjumping arena when the rider needs to change an incorrect canter lead. In itself it is a test of obedience, balance, and coordination, at the same time making the horse more supple.

Common rider/teacher faults and problems

1. The most common rider problem is failing to make a good preparation for the movement. This leads to the horse falling on its forehand and resisting so it is unable to make a smooth transition to walk and is out of balance for the next transition to canter.

2. If the rider makes a good downwards transition but hurries the upwards transition without making a clear change of aids the horse is likely to strike off with the wrong canter lead.

3. Teachers must be able to assess the horse and rider's level of training accurately so they do not demand too much too soon. If they expect this exercise to be ridden before the horse and rider are peforming a controlled and balanced canter they will spoil horse and rider confidence.

4. Teachers should build up to new exercises in stages checking the rider's understanding and ability at each stage before putting the whole exercise together.

Give and re-take the reins

a. For this movement the rider should smoothly push both hands forward towards the horse's ears so the rein contact is completely released, and then smoothly return their hands to their usual position taking up the contact as they do so.

b. The rider is asked to give and re-take the reins while in canter, to show that the horse is in self-carriage, balanced, and lightly accepting the rein contact. The rider should give and re-take the reins in one continuous movement which will last for a few canter strides.

c. The rider should check the horse's balance and acceptance of the bit by using a half-halt before they give and re-take the reins, keep riding the horse forward, and try not to lean or tip forward themselves to avoid putting the horse out of balance.

Common rider/teacher faults and problems

1. If the rider has not managed to achieve a good balanced canter with

their horse they may be inclined to give and re-take the reins in a hurried manner, snatching back the contact, and in so doing creating more resistance.

2. If the horse is not well prepared and not in self-carriage, it will be inclined to fall on its forehand and run on in canter when the contact is released.

3. If teachers do not use this exercise when helping and schooling horse and rider at home they will be missing out on a valuable way of checking and improving rider understanding and ability.

Rein back

a. In this movement the horse is asked to step back approximately three to four steps. The horse must remain straight and move its legs in diagonal pairs showing good clean steps with the feet lifted well off the floor. At the same time the horse's desire to move forward must be maintained so that having completed the movement it will move off without hesitation.

b. To ask for the rein back the rider should establish a good square halt then apply their leg aids as if asking the horse to walk forward, but keep a softly restraining rein contact, and lighten their seat. There should be no pulling or forcing, but a little help from an assistant on the ground can help the horse to understand the movement when it is first taught.

c. Rein back should only be introduced when the horse is working freely forward without resistance in all three paces.

d. A well-ridden rein back will help to engage the horse's hind quarters and lighten the forehand.

Common rider/teacher faults and problems

1. The most common rider fault is the use of strong rein aids as the rider tries to pull the horse back. This will cause resistance from the horse, a hollow outline, the quarters will swing sideways, and the horse will shuffle backwards or refuse to move at all.

2. Teachers must make sure they have made a good assessment of the horse and rider's level of training and understanding. Until a horse is moving freely forward, without resistance, it is unlikely to accept and understand the aids for rein back. At the same time, they must make sure the rider has feel and coordination so they can apply the aids sensitively. If the teacher introduces a new movement not realising that there are faults in the horse and rider's basic work they will lose their confidence and cause their work to deteriorate.

Turn on the forehand

a. In this movement the horse is asked to move its hind quarters in an arc, or half-circle, around its forehand. Its forehand remains still, while the outside foreleg steps around the inside foreleg, and the inside hind leg steps across in front of the outside hind leg as the quarters move round. The inside foreleg is lifted and replaced on the same spot, it should not remain fixed to the floor as a pivot.

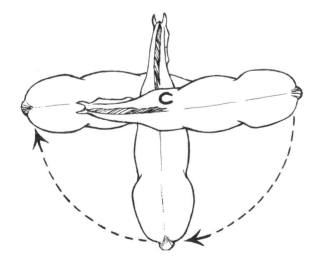

Turn on the forehand to the right

b. The horse can be asked to perform this movement from walk. The rider applies a half-halt then asks for the movement.

c. The movement can also be ridden from a halt. If a halt is used, the rider must be well prepared for the movement, so that once they have made a square halt they can ask for the movement immediately. If too much time is spent in halt, the horse is likely to "switch off" resulting in a poorly ridden turn on the forehand.

d. To ride a turn on the forehand to the right, the rider should half-halt or halt with the horse in a good outline. The inside rein (right rein) is used to indicate the direction, and ask for slight flexion at the poll so the rider can just see the horse's right eye. The inside leg (right leg) is used a little behind the girth to ask the horse to move its hind quarters over. The outside rein (left rein) keeps the horse straight, and softly restrains to prevent the horse from walking forward. The outside leg (left leg) remains on the girth and reminds the horse to keep thinking forward, and should be used to prevent the horse from stepping backwards if it tries to do so. The horse should remain in a good outline, lightly accepting the bit, throughout.

e. When the inside leg is used to move the quarters over, the position of the leg depends upon the response of the horse. Well educated responsive horses will move over when pressure is applied at the girth.

f. Although the turn on the forehand is not required in any dressage tests it is a very good coordination exercise for the rider. To ride the exercise successfully they must use each leg and hand individually, which can help them to make great improvement in their coordination.

g. The exercise also benefits the horse, as it teaches it to move away from the rider's leg. As the horse is asked to step across with its inside hind leg, bringing it further under its body, it will supple the horse, and bring its hind quarters more underneath it providing the movement is well executed.

h. As the turn on the forehand is a fairly static movement riders and teachers must make sure the horse is ridden actively forward immediately after the turn to keep the horse thinking forward.

i. The turn on the forehand can be introduced to the young horse at quite an early stage providing it has learned to accept the rider's leg aids and is moving freely forward in its basic paces.

Common rider/teacher faults and problems

1. Riders often forget the need to begin the turn from a square halt or straight and active walk. As a result the horse steps back as it turns, the rider loses control of the hind quarters, and the horse ends up more on its forehand.
2. If the rider is inexperienced they may become confused in their application of the aids which will cause great confusion for the horse.
3. Riders often try to use too much inside rein which causes the horse to bend its neck and begin walking a small circle, rather than moving its quarters over.
4. If the rider fails to use their outside rein the horse will fall out through its outside shoulder and end up making a sort of turn about its middle.
5. Riders are frequently seen with their outside leg sticking out away from the horse's side as they have completely forgotten the need to use this leg. The horse is likely to step back and once again the rider has lost control.
6. The rider may also look down and collapse towards their inside leg leading to a complete loss of position and balance which will make it very difficult for the horse to make the turn.
7. Teachers must make sure that they explain the aids very clearly and check the rider's understanding. If the teacher fails to question the rider they may find the rider thinks they understand but when it comes to riding the movement they become confused.
8. A demonstartion of how to ride a turn on the forehand will be very helpful. The teacher could also demonstrate what happens when the aids are not correctly applied.

Leg-yielding

a. This is a lateral movement in which the horse is asked to move both forwards and sideways at the same time. The horse's inside fore and hind legs will cross over and in front of the outside fore and hind.

Leg-yielding to the right in trot.

b. The movement can be ridden in walk or trot. The horse should remain in a good outline, in an active pace, and take even strides. Its body should remain straight and it should have a very slight flexion at the poll so it is looking away from the direction of the movement.

c. To ask the horse to leg-yield to the left, the rider uses their inside leg (the right leg) on or slightly behind the girth (depending on the horse's responses), to move the horse over. Their inside rein (the right rein) asks for the slight flexion at the poll so the horse looks away from the direction of the movement, and the rider can just see the horse's inside eye. The outside leg (the left leg) is used at the girth to ride the horse forward and help keep it straight. The outside rein (the left rein) controls the amount of flexion so helping to keep the horse straight.

d. The position of the inside leg varies from on, or a little behind, the girth depending on which part of the horse's body needs to be influenced more. If the forehand needs to be moved over more, then the leg is used at the girth. If the hind quarters need to be moved over more, then the leg is used behind the girth.

e. To begin with the rider can establish a good active walk then turn and ride straight along the threequarter line. Once the horse is straight some steps of leg-yield can be ridden from the threequarter line towards the boards.

f. Having ridden leg-yield on both reins in walk the rider can progress to trot which may be more difficult but will be of more benefit to the horse.

g. As the boards of the school act as a magnate to the horse, it is usually easier for the rider to practise riding from the threequarter line to the track when first riding the leg-yield. As they progress, they can practise leg-yielding from the track to the threequarter line, or in any other appropriate place in the school.

h. Although leg-yield is not required in dressage tests it is a good suppling exercise for the horse and helps to engage the hind quarters. It will also help rider coordination.

i. Leg-yield can be introduced to the young horse when it is moving freely forward in all three paces and accepting the rider's aids. If it has been introduced to turn on the forehand and learned to accept those aids it should be ready for leg-yield.

Common rider/teacher faults and problems

1. Riders often hurry into the leg-yield before making sure that their horse is straight and well prepared. This usually results in the horse just bending its neck and falling out through its outside shoulder.

2. As with the turn on the forehand, the rider may apply their inside leg and rein aids, and completely forget their outside leg and rein which should be supporting the movement. Once again the horse is likely to fall out through its outside shoulder, bend its neck and escape the movement.

3. If the horse is quite responsive to the leg aids, the rider may find themselves asking the horse to step over and forget that the horse should also move forward.

4. Teachers should demonstrate the leg-yield to help riders understand

what they are aiming to achieve. Again, the teacher could demonstrate the problems that will arise if the aids are not correctly applied.

Shoulder-in

a. In this movement the horse is asked to bend slightly around the rider's inside leg with their shoulders on an inner track so the outside foreleg is moving in line with the inside hind leg. Its inside foreleg and inside hind leg step across and in front of the outside foreleg and outside hind leg. The horse is looking slightly away from the direction in which it is moving. The horse should be moving on three tracks; the outside hind leg on one track, the inside hind and outside foreleg on a second track, and the inside foreleg on the third track.

b. This is both a suppling and collecting movement. As the legs step across and in front of each other the muscles are moved and suppled. The inside hind leg is brought underneath the horse with a lowering of the inside hip which aids engagement of the hind quarters and therefore collection.

c. The shoulder-in can be ridden in walk to begin with while both horse and rider practise, and become familiar with, the movement. It is then most effectively ridden in trot. The rider collects the trot a little, and either from a 10m circle or a well-ridden corner, brings the horse's shoulders off the track as if they were about to ride another circle. The outside rein then controls the speed and bend so the horse does not continue on the circle, but with help from the rider's inside leg begins to move down the track in the manner described above. The rider's inside leg is creating impulsion by asking the inside hind leg to step actively under the horse's body. Their outside leg is kept a little behind the girth to discourage the horse's hind quarters from swinging out. The inside rein continues to guide the horse keeping the slight flexion away from the direction in which it is moving. The rider should keep their weight evenly on both seat bones. The horse should stay in a good outline throughout, and keep the rhythm, regularity, and impulsion of the walk or trot.

d. Shoulder-in can be introduced to the horse when it is beginning to

*Shoulder-in to the
left.*

show that it can cope with a little variation within each pace, and if it
is able to leg-yield while maintaining balance and rhythm.

Common rider/teacher faults and problems

1. To begin with riders often ask for too much angle by bringing the forehand too far in off the track. This usually results in the horse swinging
   its quarters out and moving in leg-yield down the track, or leaving the
   track altogether while resisting the rider's aids.
2. Riders often allow the horse to fall out through its outside shoulder so
   the horse's forehand is not moved off the track and the horse continues
   with a bend in its neck only.

3. Because the movement is quite demanding for the horse, at first, riders often find that they lose impulsion and allow the trot to deteriorate. The horse ceases to move freely forward and the steps become irregular. Nothing is gained by horse or rider if this happens. Keeping impulsion and good rhythmical steps should be a priority.

4. A common positional fault is for the rider to collapse their inside hip and allow their weight to fall out making it difficult for the horse to keep its balance.

5. Most of the problems encountered in riding shoulder-in are due to poor coordination on the part of the rider.

6. Teachers must be observant and correct the rider's positional problems immediately so the horse has the best possible chance of performing the exercise. If the teacher stands where they can see the horse and rider coming towards them they will be able to see if the rider is sitting straight and if the horse is positioned correctly.

7. Good preparation is vital if the exercise is going to be well ridden. The teacher must insist on a good circle, and a quality trot before they allow the rider to move into shoulder-in.

Walk pirouette

a. This movement is usually ridden as a half-pirouette in which the horse's forehand is moved around its haunches.

b. The horse should mark time with its inside hind foot so it is lifted and replaced on the same spot, or slightly in front of it, with each step. The outside hind foot and both forefeet step around the inside hind. The horse should never step back.

c. Throughout the movement, which is ridden in collected walk, the horse should stay in a good outline and be slightly bent around the rider's inside leg. The sequence of footfalls, and regularity of the walk, must be maintained.

d. A well-ridden walk pirouette will aid suppleness and engagement of the hind quarters. The rider should collect the walk a little, half-halt, then softly restraining with the outside hand cease walking forward, guide the horse around their inside leg with the inside rein, maintain

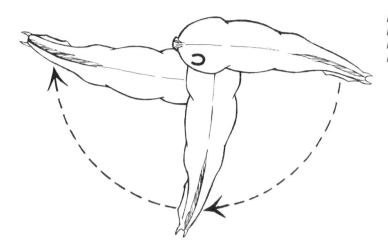

Demi-pirouette or half-turn on the haunches to the right.

impulsion with the inside leg on the girth, and use the outside leg behind the girth to prevent the quarters from swinging out.

e. Although the walk pirouette is not required in elementary dressage tests it is a useful movement to master at this level and will aid progress of horse and rider towards the next level. It is also part of the syllabus for the Stage IV riding exam.

f. It should only be introduced once the horse is showing an ability to keep balance and self-carriage through variations within each pace, and when the shoulder-in is well established.

Common rider/teacher faults and problems

1. Riders and teachers should not expect horse and rider to perform a full half-pirouette to begin with. It should be built up to by asking the horse for just one or two steps to begin with. After one or two steps ride forward and straight.
2. Riders may find themselves using their inside rein too strongly so they pull the horse around. This usually results in loss of bend around the rider's leg, the horse swinging its quarters out and becoming hollow.
3. Allowing the horse to step back is a common fault and usually the result of the rider not using their inside leg to keep the impulsion.
4. Teachers must make sure that horse and rider have reached a suitable

level in their training before attemtping to teach this movement. Remember it is not required in dressage competitions until Medium level.

Conclusion

The examiner will let you know when it is time to wind up the lesson. Try to finish on a good note and make sure you stand close to the examiner so they can hear what you say to the rider when summing up. The examiner may then discuss various aspects of the lesson with you.

Stage IV riding exam format

1. For the dressage riding candidates will usually be in a group of four. Each candidate will ride three different horses, at least one of which will be wearing a double bridle.
2. The examiners for this section will have ridden the horses early in the morning before the candidates ride them. Therefore they know if they are easy, difficult, stiff, or a joy to ride. The examination centre will also have provided the examiners with notes about each horse's age and level of training, along with any little "quirks" or good points they have. This helps the examiners to assess the riding ability of each candidate when they see how they get on with these horses.
3. For each horse the candidates will be given a brief so they have a particular aim with that horse. They may be asked to ride and assess the horse to find out about its level of training and its good and bad points. They could be asked to work on shortening and lengthening working up to lateral work for Elementary level. They may be asked to work on the horse's walk and canter then work towards simple change and counter-canter. The examiner will decide on the briefs to be given on the day.
4. Candidates will be asked to finish the piece of work they are riding and will then be questioned about the horses they have just ridden. They are likely to be asked about its paces, whether it had any problems, what level of training it may have achieved, how they would hope to improve it in future, and so on.

5. Before mounting each horse the candidate should remember to check the age of the horse and look at its overall conformation and muscle development. This should help them to assess the horse's abilities.

6. The examiners are looking for capable and experienced riders who show a good understanding of all the subject matter covered in this chapter and an ability to apply it effectively. They would like to see the candidates demonstrate that they can use a good plan of work for each horse and correctly assess its paces, way of going, and any problems. When discussing the horses with the candidates they would like to hear answers that show knowledge and a good understanding of the horse and its abilities.

Common rider/teacher faults and problems

1. In both the Stage IV riding and the teaching exam candidates often fail to work horses and riders to a suitable level. When riding, they may work the horse quite well in its basic paces, but not progress to ask for more demanding work that it is capable of. When teaching they may improve the horse and rider combination so they are working quite well, but not work on more demanding exercises that they would have been capable of. Therefore they have not really assessed the horse or horse and rider combination at the correct level.

2. Stage IV riding candidates sometimes work the horses in a very fragmented way. They don't appear to have a progressive plan, and fail to work up to exercises so the horse is not well prepared and therefore does not perform well. This shows a lack of experience at this level.

3. In both the riding and teaching exams when examiners discuss the work with the candidates they find that what they say seems to bear little relation to what the examiners have seen. This usually shows a lack of understanding and experience on the part of the candidate.

Helpful hints on exam technique

1. When talking to the examiner about the horses you have ridden in the Stage IV exam, it can be helpful to use an acronym to remind you of all the information you would like to give the examiner. An example of an

acronym is PORTBALL which is made up of letters which stand for key words to do with the way the horse was working. This acronym can help you to summarise the horse's work in a logical and informative way, which can be very helpful when you are under the strain of exam conditions.

P   = paces
O   = outline
R   = rhythm
T   = tempo
B   = balance
A   = acceptance of the aids
L   = lateral work
L   = level of training

These are just key words to help you. Obviously, other information can be given, and you can use other key words and make up an acronym of your own.

2. An acronym could also help you when discussing the horse you worked with in the dressage lesson.

3. Practise talking about horses and riders and their way of working, their good and bad points and problems. Really think about what you are saying. Too often candidates give meaningless answers or assessments. Try not to use sentences like, "He had a really nice trot." This doesn't really tell the examiner a great deal. A better comment would be, "He had a really good trot with plenty of impulsion, rhythm, and a good long stride."

4. Make sure you don't fall into the trap of saying, for example: "I would have liked to try some counter-canter." The examiner may say, "Why didn't you?" Candidates often say they would use a particular exercise or would have liked to try an exercise which in fact they had plenty of time and every opportunity to do. Talk about what you did do and then go on to say, for example: "When I had worked him for a little longer and produced a better trot, then I would like to go on to this exercise."

5. As with all sections of the exam, remember when your rider is staionary and you are explaining or discussing a point to stand near to the examiner so they can hear your discussions and explanations.

3　The Jumping Lesson

In general

Jumping lessons can take many different forms. They can be conducted in an indoor school, an outdoor manege, a field, or a cross-country area. Lessons may include grid work, single fences, a course of fences, or a combination of any or all of these.

Exam format

a. Each candidate is given approximately 35 minutes for the jumping lesson.

b. A horse and rider combination will be provided, capable of jumping fences up to Novice Horse Trials and Newcomers showjumping height.

c. It may be that the horse and rider are competing at or above this level, or aiming towards this level in their future competitions. The examiner will have been informed about the horse and rider's ability and will give the candidate a brief suited to that particular partnership.

d. In general the brief will be to work on improving the horse's jumping technique using the fences provided, and to improve the rider's influence on the horse.

e. A ready-built course of fences will be provided, but you can make whatever changes you like. The examiner would like to see you use the fences in a constructive manner showing a good understanding of fence building, distances, and safety.

f. You will usually be sharing an arena with another candidate giving a jumping lesson, each of you having a set of jumps to use. So you need to show that you are aware of the other rider and make sure your pupil does not interrupt the other lesson.

Introduction

a. You should introduce yourself in the usual way, and find out all you can about the horse and rider. How old is the horse? What competitive experience has it had? Is it wearing its usual tack? What are the rider's aims, what competitive experience has he or she had, have they passed any equestrian exams, do they usually ride and compete on this horse?

b. Make a quick check of their tack while you are talking to them, then ask them to go and work in for jumping so you can have a look at them as a horse and rider partnership. They will already be partly worked-in so you can progress quite quickly.

c. While they are working in you can watch and assess them whilst also having a look at the fences.

Content

1. The subject matter of your lesson will obviously depend upon the weak and strong points you find in the horse and rider combination you are teaching. You may include any of the work from the following section, bearing in mind that you only have a short amount of time.

2. The general format to follow will begin with the use of a cross-pole from trot, progressing to an upright from trot to canter. Gradually go on to jump a selection of single fences, then link some of the fences together before going on to jump a course.

3. Having jumped a course of fences you may need to repeat parts or all of the course having made further corrections, so you can show further improvement.

Subject matter for lessons to Novice horse trials and Newcomers level

The rider

a. At this level of showjumping it is easy to assume that the rider has an established and balanced position. However, as this is not always the case, it is important to spend some time assessing the rider's position and ability to apply the aids when at jumping length.

b. I think it is better to avoid using the term "jumping position". There is no real set position for the rider to adopt when jumping as the position of the rider is, or should be, fluently and constantly changing as they ride over fences. They will also be tackling a variety of fences which will need changes of position and balance.

c. It is necessary to practise a forward position, or forward seat, or jumping seat, whichever term you prefer. This forward position may be used when the rider prepares the horse for jumping, approaches a fence, rides across country, and when galloping. The degree of forwardness will vary according to each situation, but should incorporate a lightening of the seat. The rider may just be slightly out of the saddle just taking their weight off the horse's back with only the slightest incline forward with their upper body. At the other extreme the rider may be folded right forward close to the horse's neck, a position demonstrated by flat race jockeys in particular.

d. With stirrups at the shorter jumping length the rider should be seen to remain balanced and effective. The rider's lower leg position is most important. Their legs should be by the girth, in contact with the horse's sides, and with their weight in their heels. Their legs should remain still and secure.

e. The rider's upper body must remain in balance whether they are sitting in the saddle or lightening their seat and moving into a forward position.

f. Above all, the rider must learn to be effective when riding with shorter stirrups in preparation for jumping, and must be completely in balance and independent of the reins.

g. To improve balance and effectiveness, plenty of work on the flat and outside over varying terrain, in forward position, is helpful along with using grids as gymnastic jumping exercises.

Common rider/teacher faults and problems

1. Riders and teachers must continue to pay as much attention to the

application of the aids and the horse's way of going as they did when working on improving their dressage. There is a tendency to treat jumping as a completely separate activity, when it should be thought of as a continuation of the dressage work. As with all riding, if the rider is sitting badly, out of balance, and applying the aids incorrectly, the horse cannot be expected to work fluently and well.

2. Teachers must remember that their pupils need to practise riding with a shorter stirrup length. It is not helpful to ask riders to adjust their stirrups just before jumping. They should work in and school their horses with shorter stirrups prior to a jumping session. In this way they are practising using different muscles and becoming effective when riding with jumping length stirrups.

3. Teachers often forget to correct the obvious. Remember, if the horse and rider make a good turn to the fence, followed by a balanced and active approach, the jump itself is likely to go well. Look at the quality of turns and approaches and work to improve them.

Pole work

a. Both horse and rider can continue to benefit from the use of pole work in their everyday training, whatever their level of competitive achievement. Poles can be used to improve balance, suppleness, and coordination.

b. Trotting poles, especially those that are raised up to about 45mm or so off the ground, encourage the horse to flex its joints and therefore aid suppleness. The horse's balance will improve as it needs to have its hind quarters engaged in order to keep its rhythm and tempo. It is also a good way of introducing jumping and poles into a training session rather than suddenly surprising the horse with a jump. In this way poles can help to build confidence. Trotting poles should be placed 1.4–1.5m apart for an average horse.

c. Over trotting poles the rider can also feel the more elevated steps which can help them to feel what they are looking for in a more collected and active pace. It will also improve their balance as they need to make subtle adjustments to keep with the horse as it works over the

Horse and rider working over raised trotting poles.

poles. Rider confidence will also benefit with a gradual introduction to jumping giving them time to practise turns, approaches, and feel in tune with the horse's attitude.

d. However, trotting poles can be dangerous if misused. A rushing horse may attempt to canter, or jump, over the poles. If it lands on a pole it could be injured or fall and injure itself and the rider.

e. Single ground poles can be placed at random around the school to help an anxious horse to become familiar with trotting over poles.

f. Horse and rider combinations that are relaxed and familiar with ground poles and trotting poles may benefit from the use of placing poles used in front of a fence, approximately 3m away. These can be very helpful when horse and rider need to gain confidence in their ability to judge their take-off point.

Common rider/teacher faults and problems

1. Teachers sometimes forget the importance of making sure that riders are aware of the dangers as well as the benefits of pole work. Riders must realise that a horse rushing over poles may tread or jump on the poles, possibly causing it to fall and injure itself. By becoming aware, at this level, the rider learns to take some responsibility for turning the horse away from the poles if the horse is not approaching in a calm and active way.

2. Riders must approach poles with as much care as they would when approaching a jump. They should aim to make an accurate turn, in a balanced and active pace, followed by a purposeful get-away along a planned track and not allow the horse to fall in and lose balance.

3. Teachers should always build up to exercises gradually. Using a placing pole in front of a jump when you don't know the horse and rider can be dangerous. Some horses try to jump placing pole and jump all in one which could lead to an accident for horse and rider.

4. Some teachers use the same exercises and distances whatever the horse and whatever the problem. This may help some combinations, but be detrimental to others. A teacher should always have a clear idea of what they are trying to achieve then use relevant exercises to reach that aim.

(*Note*: Due to limited time and the need for examiners to see that each candidate is capable of helping the rider over a course of fences in preparation for competition, there is not usually time to work over poles in the Intermediate Teaching Test.)

Grid work

a. All horses and riders will benefit from working through grids. They help to make horse and rider more agile, develop a feel for stride and take-off point, teach horse and rider to make quick and fluent adjustments to keep in balance, and build up their confidence.

b. Many different combinations of fences, poles and distances can be used depending on the stride length of the horse and ability of horse and rider. Great care must be taken to adjust distances and the combinations of poles and fences according to horse and rider ability to make sure they are not "over faced" or asked the impossible. In general, keeping to slightly shorter distances helps the horse to round over its fences and keep its hind quarters engaged.

c. A simple grid may include a placing pole followed by a cross-pole 3m away. Then a small upright 6.5–7m beyond the cross-pole, then a small spread another 7m beyond that.

d. Again, it is very important that the teacher has a clear idea of what he or she is hoping to achieve. They should build up gradually from a single pole to a line of fences. Remember, when you increase the height of the fences substantially you will need to lengthen the distances a little for the horse to have room for landing, taking a stride and taking off again. At the same time, if you have the distance too long coming into a spread fence the horse will already be stretching before jumping the fence and will be unable to stretch far enough to clear the spread.

Common rider/teacher faults and problems

1. The position of the grid in the arena needs careful consideration. If schooling in an indoor school with one open side, the grid should be placed by the closed side in case of horses ducking out and unseating a rider over the edge of the school. If the school is wide enough the grid can be placed centrally so approaches can be made from both reins. If there are mirrors in the school, care must be taken not to jump horses directly towards them in case the horse becomes confused by the mirror image. There must always be plenty of room for both approach and landing. It is not a good idea to jump straight towards the exit. Teachers must assess the best position for the grid according to the school area they are working in.

2. Riders must be careful to ride good approaches and get-aways. There is a tendency for the rider to concentrate on the grid but allow the horse to fall in and be unbalanced on approach and/or collapse on landing, forgetting to ride away and re-establish a balanced and active pace.

3. Teachers also sometimes fail to look at how the horse and rider are approaching or riding away from the grid. As a result they may miss seeing the cause of problems that occur.

4. It is easy to end up repeatedly jumping a grid to try to improve a particular problem, at the same time forgetting how many jumping efforts the horse is making each time. This can be very tiring for the horse and cause it to begin making mistakes. Grid work then becomes detrimental. Teachers must make sure they do not overdo the exercise.

5. When a teacher or rider is lacking in experience they may misunderstand why a horse is behaving in a certain way, and try to treat the symptom rather than the cause. For example, if a horse rushes away from its fences, it will be due to a lack of balance and maybe fear, especially if it is a young or inexperienced horse. This problem cannot be corrected by trying to reprimand or steady the horse after the fence; the approach and jump themselves need to be practised before improvement can be made and then the horse will move away steadily after the fence.

(*Note*: Due to lack of time it will not be possible to jump a grid during the individual jumping lesson of the Intermediate Teaching Test. The examiner needs to see that you can give a lesson which will help a rider with jumping a course of fences at a competition.)

Jumping a course of showjumping fences

a. Introducing horse and rider to jumping a course of showjumping fences, or improving their current technique, can be done with the use of a few fences thoughtfully positioned in the arena.

b. By placing fences fairly close together in the middle of the arena, and building some of them so they can be jumped from both sides exercises can be built up gradually incorporating more fences as horse and rider improve.

c. It is important to make all approaches straightforward, so that if they are well ridden the horse and rider can meet the fence on a good line and in a good pace. Courses should not be "trappy" with awkward approaches. Several changes of rein will help to keep horse and rider

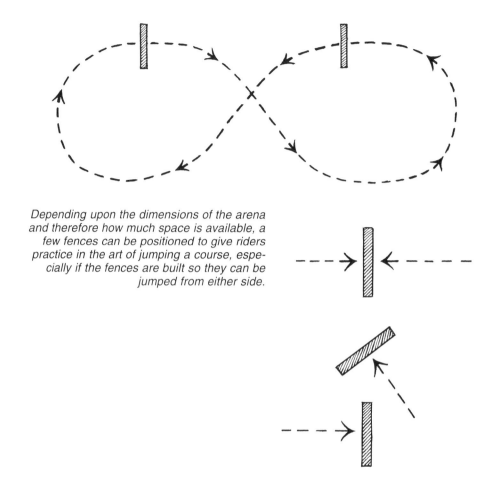

Depending upon the dimensions of the arena and therefore how much space is available, a few fences can be positioned to give riders practice in the art of jumping a course, especially if the fences are built so they can be jumped from either side.

thinking ahead, but each change of rein should be easily achievable if the rider is planning and riding well.

d. Teach the rider to make good use of the arena to give themselves more time and aid a balanced approach. If they cut corners and allow the horse to fall in on turns each fence begins to appear too quickly and they will not be able to cope with the course.

e. Emphasise the need to remember and apply all the dressage work horse and rider have done when riding between the fences and check that the rider is achieving a good balanced position over the fence.

f. Young horses and novice riders should be asked to trot round a course of small fences before they try to approach in canter. Less mistakes are made in trot and everything happens a little more slowly. Providing the fences are small they will find trot easier to cope with at first.

g. Canter approaches are needed when horse and rider are becoming more competitive. Not only are the fences bigger, but there will be a time limit after which time faults will be incurred. Horse and rider need some practice in keeping a flowing canter with impulsion, balance and rhythm around a course of fences.

h. By incorporating some related distances into a course of fences you can help a rider to improve his or her feel for the quality of the canter needed when jumping a course. A related distance is when two fences are further apart than those in a combination, but still a set number of

Rider in a good balanced forward position in flight over a fence.

strides apart (up to five strides). A horse's stride length is approximately equal to 3.5–4m. Having taken eleven human strides to set out a two-stride distance, you can add four more strides for each extra horse stride required. Alternatively, estimate the approximate point at which the horse will land from the fence (approximately two human strides), then measure the distance by taking four human strides for each horse stride. If the rider knows how many strides they are aiming for between fences it may help them to ride either more actively forward on a lazy horse, or more steadily on a flat and rushing horse.

i. Related distances can also be used in training exercises for horse and rider. The rider can be asked to ride four, five, or six strides between the same two fences in order to improve their ability to shorten or lengthen the horse's stride while keeping the quality of the pace so the horse can still jump the fences cleanly.

Common rider/teacher faults and problems

1. When riding a course most mistakes are made between fences. Teachers must be very observant and correct riders firmly when they fail to ride good turns, or choose poor lines to fences.

2. Some teachers try to say too much when a rider is actually riding the course of fences. The rider has so much to think about at this time they are unlikely to hear any corrections. It is better for the teacher to note the problems, wait for the rider to finish the exercise, then go through the areas that need improvement and send the rider away on another exercise to try and improve each point.

3. If the rider is nervous or struggling with the exercise set they will often lose their way around a course or miss one or more of the fences. This shows they are not yet ready for the task set; a more simple exercise should be used to avoid the rider losing confidence through their being pushed beyond their abilities.

4. Riders often begin the course well but then, through ineffective riding, gradually let the horse get long and flat so the last part of the course is full of mistakes. Teachers should help the rider identify where their technique needs improvement.

5. Combination fences may pose particular problems for some riders. If the rider is getting left behind on take-off they will hinder the horse and make it difficult for the horse to make the distance between the fences. The same will apply if the rider gets in front of the horse and puts it out of balance between the fences. It may be that the rider has failed to establish a good active pace on approach, or that the horse finds the distance too long or too short for its stride. More often than not it is due to rider error. Teachers need to be able to correctly identify the problem so they can work on putting it right. It may be necessary to go back to grid work, improve the rider's dressage work, or adjust the distance to make it easier before making it a more realistic distance again.

Conclusion

The examiner will give you a warning when it is time to bring the lesson to a close. As with all the lessons, stand close to the examiner while you are summing up and asking your rider if they have any questions. The examiner may like to ask you some questions about the lesson and find out your opinion as to whether or not the horse and rider are ready to go on and compete at the level they are aiming for.

Cross-country jumping

(Note: Cross-country jumping is not taught in the Intermediate Teaching Test but will be discussed in the theory section. Those taking the riding section of the Stage IV exam will ride over cross-country fences.)

a. Safety of horse and rider must be uppermost when teaching in general, but particularly when teaching cross-country riding. Riders should always wear body protectors and horses should wear protective boots. The safety of the location chosen should also be considered. An enclosed field or area of woodland is best, and there should be more than one experienced escort especially if the teaching session is located away from the home base.

b. There are many different types of cross-country fences. To begin with the teacher should aim to introduce horse and rider to small fences of each different type. The horse and rider may be capable of jumping larger fences, but until they have gained experience in negotiating the particular questions asked by different types of cross-country fence they should not be asked to tackle anything big.

c. The sort of fences they will need experience of include drops, light into dark, water complexes, coffins, banks, trakehners, steps, ski-jumps, and corners – to name just a few.

d. Teachers need to help the rider understand how the horse may react to different fences and then, using a small fence of a particular type, let them experience the problems for themselves. As long as the fence is small, horse and rider will be able to cope with any problems they encounter without losing confidence – which would not be the case if it was a big fence.

e. The trakehner fence, for example, should be approached in a strong but not too long canter as the horse will tend to begin shortening when it suddenly sees the ditch. The rider must feel that he or she has plenty of horse in front of them so they can keep the horse's hind quarters underneath its body and ride it confidently forward giving the horse the confidence to continue.

f. A coffin needs a short and bouncy canter approach so the horse has plenty of impulsion but time to see what it is being asked to do. If it can see that it has a jump and room to land before the ditch it should feel confident enough to go on. However, the shorter and bouncier the canter the more the rider needs to be there with their legs to make sure the horse does go on.

g. For a drop fence the approach shouldn't be a too fast, nor should it be a too short, stride. If the stride is very short the horse will drop vertically down making the descent very steep. If the rider aims for a slightly lengthening stride the horse will jump out more and have a less steep descent. The rider needs to sit back but allow the horse freedom of head and neck without losing the contact. They must be ready to let the reins slip a little and then take them up again quickly on landing.

h. There are times when a trot approach may be needed. For example, coming into a steep ski-jump or steps going down. The rider must remember, when going more slowly a lot of leg is needed to make sure horse and rider keep going.

Common rider/teacher faults and problems

1. Riders can get very unbalanced across country. There is a tendency for them to stand in their stirrups and tip forward. Teachers must take time to work with riders around fields and through woodland practising a balanced forward position in which their weight is off the horse's back but over its centre of gravity. Their lower legs must be underneath them with weight in their heels and the legs completely secure so they can use them effectively.

2. Horses galloping across country looking long and flat between fences are an all too common sight. The rider then leaves it until the last minute to try and get the horse between leg and hand again. As a result the horse is often fighting the rider when approaching the fence which is a recipe for disaster. Riders must learn to keep the horse together with hind quarters engaged at all times.

3. Tired riders and horses are quite likely to have accidents. It is very important that both are fit enough for the task ahead.

4. As with any aspect of equestrianism horse and rider need to gain as much experience at the lower levels as possible before moving on to bigger and more technical courses. It is vital that any problems encountered at the lower levels are noted and worked on before moving on. If they are not sorted out in the early stages they will lead to problems later just as they would in dressage or showjumping. Unfortunately, with cross-country riding the consequences are usually more dramatic and likely to cause injury to horse and rider.

Jumping on the lunge

In the early stages of training, jumping the young horse on the lunge can be helpful.

a. Suitable equipment is needed. Apart from the usual lungeing equipment, blocks or very small stands are required to allow the lunge line to be moved freely with the horse over the fence. An assistant must be available to move poles and put up jumps.

b. The trainer must make sure the horse on the lunge works evenly on both reins.

c. Jumping on the lunge is a way of introducing the horse to poles and jumps without a rider on its back. The horse can look and jump and find its balance without the added problem of coping with the rider's weight.

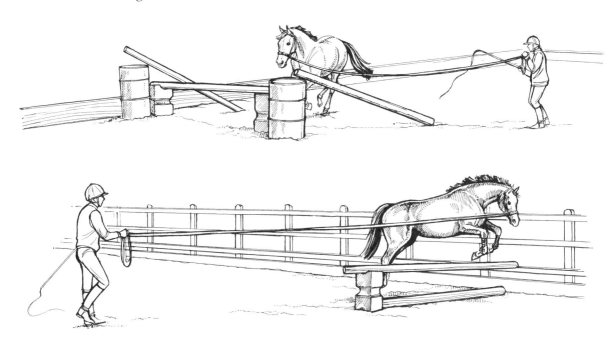

Jumping on the lunge using blocks and poles that allow the lunge line to move freely with the horse.

d. When first introduced to jumping the horse may hesitate, leap awkwardly, jump very high, and generally act unpredictably. This makes it very difficult for the rider to keep in balance and not hinder the horse. Lunge jumping can be a way around this problem.

e. However, if jumping on the lunge is not performed expertly, it will be detrimental to the horse. Most trainers will use loose jumping in a jumping lane or indoor school if they have these facilities rather than lungeing the horse over jumps.

Common faults and problems

1. In order to make sure that the horse has a straight approach and get-away from the jump the trainer must run along beside the horse and not bring it around on to a circle too soon after jumping. This would cause the horse to lose balance, probably knock in to itself, and then lose confidence in the whole idea. The trainer must make sure the horse has completed the jump and regained its balance. Failure to do so will adversely affect its jumping technique, causing it to hollow and lose balance.

2. When the trainer runs along beside the horse to give it a straight approach and get-away his or her action can worry the horse and cause it to rush as it begins to think it is being chased into the jump.

3. Lungeing is a demanding task when carried out on the flat, but when jumps are included it requires great expertise and attention to safety if it is to be done effectively. The trainer should spend plenty of time in practising the lungeing of horses over poles before moving on to jumping.

Stage IV jumping exam format

1. Each candidate will ride two horses in the jumping section of the Stage IV. One horse will be ridden over a course of showjumping fences up to a height of 1m 7cm, and the other over a course of cross-country fences, usually no more than about 1m in height.

2. You will be given an opportunity to walk both the showjumping and the cross-country fences before the exam begins.

3. You should treat the jumping of each horse as a schooling session, and not as if you were jumping a course of fences at a competition.

4. You will be given warming-up time and warm-up fences to work over. While warming-up you will be riding with the other candidates in

your group and should show that you are capable of doing so safely and thoughtfully, just as you would if warming-up in a collecting ring at a competition.

5. The examiners are looking to see that you are an effective and experienced rider. They may discuss the horse's work with you and would like to hear knowledgeable answers and suggestions for exercises that may help the horse improve in the future.

6. You may have problems with one or both of the horses. This does not necessarily mean you have done anything wrong, the examiners will be looking to see how you cope with the problems. They would like to see harmonious work showing balance, tact and fluency.

Common rider faults and problems

1. Most problems arise through a lack of experience on the part of the candidate. You must be used to jumping a variety of horses over fences of the required height on a regular basis, otherwise you will be out of practice and unfamiliar with the balance and technique required at this level. If you have not been jumping a variety of horses there could be problems you may encounter for the first time with horses in this examination.

2. Remember to check the tack, and look at the overall type, muscle development, fitness and conformation, of both the horses allocated to you. Don't forget to make an assessment of the horses' age. All these points are often forgotten, but they are relevant to the way the individual horse may be expected to work for you.

3. When riding the course the most common problems include poor judgement of pace, inability to keep the horse between leg and hand in a balanced canter, and poor approaches to fences from a badly-ridden track. The rider may also have positional problems leading to lack of balance, interference with the horse as it jumps, and a general lack of harmony and effectiveness.

Helpful hints on exam technique

1. When teaching the individual jumping lesson do make sure you check each of the fences before you ask the rider to jump them, and check the

distances between related fences. Although the course will have been built correctly to begin with, other candidates will have used the fences during the day. They may have made adjustments that are not suitable for your lesson, or have left the course with an empty jump cup or poles incorrectly placed and so on. Make sure each fence is safe before you use it.

2. Try not to spend too much time moving fences. There will be someone to assist you, but it should not be necessary to move fences around. Your time is limited, so make adjustments but don't move fences unless it is really vital to the achievement of your aims.

3. Many candidates get stuck working over one fence and end up making the horse worse rather than better. Take care not to jump your warm-up fence too many times. The aim is to help the rider with jumping a course of fences with that particular horse. Moving on to other fences will often improve the horse by giving it more to think about.

4. If you would like to use a placing pole to help the horse and rider, always ask the rider if they are familiar with working over placing poles with that particular horse. Some horses have a tendency to jump placing pole and jump as one – which could be dangerous – so check with the rider first.

5. Although you do not need to make the fences any bigger than about 1m, you must be careful not to keep the fences so small that the horse and rider are never really presented with a challenge. Your pupil may sail around a course of 90cm fences with style and balance, but lose their poise and control for a variety of reasons over larger fences. If you do not build a course to a suitable height, you will be unable to assess the ability of your pupil. Obviously, you shouldn't put up large fences if the horse and rider are not capable. This is why you must have sufficient experience at this level, so you can make an accurate assessment.

4 The Lunge Lesson

In general

Lungeing can be of great value to both horse and rider.It is used in the early training of the horse before it is backed and ridden and in the early training of riders, often before they are able to ride independently. Lungeing then goes on being a useful way of improving both horse and rider in different ways throughout their training.

Lungeing the horse

a. Before a young horse is backed, lungeing is used to: teach a series of commands by which we can communicate with the horse; familiarise the horse with different items of tack; help the horse develop its muscles and balance in preparation for accepting a rider on its back.

b. As the horse matures, and is backed and ridden, the use of the lunge is continued as a form of exercise and sometimes to help correct problems. Working the horse actively on a circle is intensive work – 20 minutes on the lunge can be equal to one hour's ridden work. Lungeing the horse once a week can help in the managment of a busy routine, helping to reduce the time taken to exercise all the horses in a yard for example. Lungeing is also useful if a horse has a back injury or muscle strain that may require short periods of work, without a rider, to help an effective recovery programme.

c. For lungeing to be effective it must be carried out expertly. It is a skill that takes many hours of practice to achieve and should be looked upon as a way of riding the horse from the ground.

d. First, when the horse is sent out on to the circle, obedience should be considered. Unless the horse is so fresh that it is likely to kick and buck, putting the person lungeing at risk, it should be asked to walk out on to the circle, moving away from that person calmly. If you were riding the horse, you would not tolerate it trotting away the minute you sat in the saddle, so, in the same way, you do not tolerate the horse rushing off into trot the minute you let it out on the lunge. However, for the sake of safety, you may need to let a very fresh horse move off quickly, then bring it forward to walk and start again when it is in a calmer frame of mind and ready to pay attention.

e. As the person lungeing, you should never back away from the horse as this will only encourage it to come towards you, causing a loss of control. You should walk forward with the horse, keeping level with its shoulder, and gradually let the horse move away from you, encouraging it to do so with both voice and lunge whip. In fact, if the horse does fall in or come towards you, you should move towards it, at the same time pushing it forward more. This will encourage it to go forward and out on to a larger circle.

f. While sending the horse out on the circle, it is essential to keep a good steady contact on the lunge line. Each time you lose contact you are losing control. When the person lungeing is not really in control the horse will be slow to respond to all the commands, particularly those for downwards transitions. The horse can be seen jogging on for several circles in trot before it eventually walks, and then continues slowly in walk for several circles before it finally goes forward to halt, often turning in towards the person lungeing as it does so. These actions of the horse are all signs of the person lungeing being ineffective and out of control.

g. Once the horse is on the circle, maintain contact with the lunge line and keep yourself positioned opposite, or just behind, the horse's shoulder. Use your voice, backed up by the lunge whip as necessary, to give the commands. Just as when you ride the horse you give aids to prepare for different movements and transitions, so, you now use your voice to prepare the horse, and give the aids, on the lunge. Keep commands simple and consistent to avoid confusion.

h. The horse should be worked actively forward into a contact with the side reins (which may be attached once the horse has worked-in), in a good outline, being asked to track up in trot and remain steady and balanced in canter.

i. The size of the circle used can be varied but remember that constant circle work is strenuous and it is preferable to keep the circle at around 18–20m diameter. As the person lungeing the horse, you can walk a small circle in the middle of the circle but be careful not to wander as the horse may catch you off balance or you may encourage crooked-ness or a lack of balance in the horse.

j. The person lungeing needs to practise standing and moving in a bal-nced manner. For example, if you are lungeing on the left rein, your right leg should step forward and around your left leg, and *vice versa* on the right rein. If you remain in balance you can move with the horse easily if it pulls or shoots off, or you can stand your ground if the horse gets strong. It is advisable to remove spurs before lungeing in case you trip yourself up!

k. Always wear gloves for lungeing to protect your hands and to aid grip. It is advisable, too, to wear a hard hat as young, fit, or excited horses can easily fly-buck and kick out at head height.

l. Do not put the whip on the ground if you can possibly avoid doing so. When you bend down to pick up the whip, the horse might easily mis-interpret your move and think that you are going to hit it. The horse could shoot off and catch you off balance or may just take advantage of the situation.

m. The key to effective lungeing is to treat it as if you were riding the horse. You are simply using a different set of aids but are looking for the same qualities in the horse's work. The horse should go freely and actively forward, keeping a rhythm and remaining straight and bal-anced in a good outline.

Stage IV Lungeing exam format

1. In the riding section of the Stage IV exam, candidates are required to lunge a horse for about 20 minutes. They should demonstrate that they: have experience of lungeing horses effectively; can assess and develop the horse's paces; can use ground poles if necessary to improve the

horse; can discuss the horse and suggest future work for it; and can use and handle lungeing equipment safely.

2. The horses will usually have been worked-in for the candidates in advance, or the individual candidate will be lungeing a horse that one of the other candidates has been working before them.

3. The space given to each horse will be no less than 20m square and is often a larger area.

4. The horses may be tacked up with saddles and bridles, but as they are not being ridden they will often have lungeing rollers on instead of saddles. This will depend upon the centre where the examination is being held and the equipment that is available.

Content

1. When you are allocated a horse try to find out its name as this will help you communicate with it. Quickly but thoroughly check all tack and equipment, making any adjustments you think necessary. Do not hesitate to ask for assistance if, for example, part of the equipment is faulty. Make sure you check the age of the horse as this will have a bearing on how it can be expected to work on the lunge. You may be given anything from a 3-year-old to a mature and experienced horse, so have a quick look at its teeth. Conformation and muscle development of the horse will also tell you something about its way of going and the level of its training, so don't forget to observe and make a mental note of this.

2. When you begin lungeing remember you are quite likely to be sharing a school area with one or more other horses on the lunge. Be aware of not cracking your whip, which may upset others, and make transitions, especially those into canter, away from the other horses to minimise the chances of upsetting their work.

3. As you work the horse you should be aware of all the points mentioned above regarding lungeing the horse. Imagine yourself riding the horse and think of how you would be trying to improve its way of going. Is it active enough? Is it working in a round outline with hocks engaged? Is it obedient to the aids? Is it straight on the circle? Is it balanced in trot and canter and through its transitions? Is it more supple

on one rein than on the other? These are all points you should be working to impove.

4. You are expected to work the horse in canter. However, if you find the horse is very unbalanced in canter and feel the work is detrimental to the horse, you should not continue. You need to be experienced enough to assess the horse correctly.

5. Ground poles are available for you to use. You do not have to use them, but if you feel you could improve the horse by doing so then an assistant will lay out the poles according to your instructions. Make sure you have reasons and aims for the pole work.

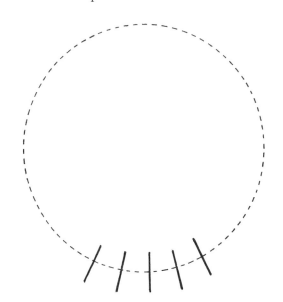

On a circle the poles can be laid out in a fan shape. This makes the poles easy to incorporate into the circle work.

6. Finally, the examiner will discuss the session with you. They would like to hear an accurate assessment of the horse's work and some ideas for improving or helping the horse in future work sessions.

Common candidate faults and problems

1. Many candidates do not seem to have progressed from the lungeing requirements of the Stage III exam. You must make sure you lunge a

variety of different types of horse frequently. It is only through regular practice that you will become efficient and effective in your handling of the equipment, and be able to develop a feel for improving and helping horses on the lunge.

2. When asking horses to canter on the lunge candidates often fail to establish a good forward going and balanced trot. The horse then finds it difficult to canter and explodes into the pace bucking and kicking. This upsets other horses in the school and does nothing to help the candidate with control and communication. Make sure the horse is balanced and ready to canter just as you would when riding.

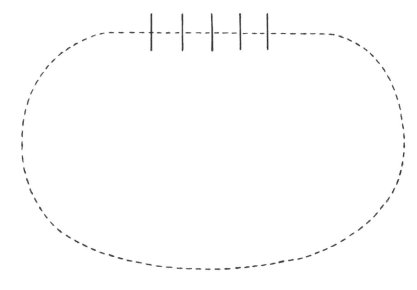

If the poles are arranged in a straight line the lunger must take care to move the horse on to a straight line before approaching the poles. Keep the horse straight over the poles, and then continue in a straight line after the poles to make sure the horse is balanced before moving on to a circle again.

3. Lack of experience often leads to the candidate being unaware of whether the horse is following the line of the circle. The horse may be crooked, falling-in on some parts of the circle, moving off at a tangent to follow the edge of the school, and so on. The candidate does nothing to improve these points and the horse's work deteriorates. Again, this

is due to a lack of practice – and therefore feel – for the way the horse is working.

4. When candidates fail to look at conformation and muscle development or check the horse's age before they begin, they may find themselves being too demanding of a young horse, causing it to tire and the work to deteriorate. They may find themselves with a more mature horse that is basically obedient and end up simply letting it move round them in circles without really asking it to work towards improvement. Do check on the age of the horse and consider its conformation. Heavier, more "cobby" horses will find working on the lunge more difficult and tiring.

Lungeing the rider

a. Lungeing is an excellent way of improving the rider's basic position, balance, feel, and depth of seat. It can be of great help from beginner level upwards.

b. It is very important to have a horse which is experienced in the job of lungeing. Such a horse must have good smooth paces, and also be well-balanced, even-tempered, and obdient to the aids. A horse which is too exuberant can be difficult for the person lungeing to control; he or she needs to be able to concentrate more on the rider than the horse. Likewise, a horse which is lazy and needs to be chased, gives the person lungeing too much to do and makes the paces very inconsistent and jerky for the rider.

c. It is also very important to have a well-designed saddle that is of the correct size and type for the rider. Beginners and very novice riders need a comfortable general purpose saddle that is not too forward cut. More advanced riders need a dressage saddle to help them develop a deeper seat and longer leg position.

d. Once riders have progressed beyond the beginner level the main aim of lunge lessons is to improve their feel, suppleness, depth of seat, balance and, therefore, their influence over their horses.

e. The teacher needs to be experienced in observing the rider on the lunge. He or she should be able to see if a rider is tense in any part of their body and, if so, to help the rider to relax. They should be able to see if the rider is out of balance with the horse, trying to maintain an incorrect position, and be able to correct their position and put them in balance with the horse. They should be able to see if the rider loses balance or becomes tense during transitions, and be able to work towards improvement of this problem.

f. By working the horse through transitions from one pace to another, or into halt and forward to walk or trot again, or through transitions within the pace (whilst looking for and improving all the problems discussed immediately above), the teacher should be able to make great steps towards improving the rider's feel for the horse and influence over the horse when riding independently.

g. To begin with the teacher can be in complete control of the horse and all the transitions made. The rider just concentrates on correcting and improving themselves. The teacher should then instruct the rider to apply some of the aids themselves, to see if they can maintain any improvement they have shown. In this way the rider is better prepared for riding independently of the lunge at a later stage.

Lunge lesson exam format

Each candidate is given approximately 25 minutes to give the lunge lesson. The horse provided will be an experienced lunge horse and should already have been worked-in. A rider, of up to Stage III level, will also be provided and may be a competition rider, a Stage III student working for Stage IV, or a rider of slightly lower standard working towards general improvement.

Introduction

1. You should introduce yourself to the pupil in the usual way. Find out about their riding experience and aims. Ask if they have ever had a lunge lesson before and if they have been lunged before on this particular horse.

2. Make sure you explain to the pupil what you intend to ask them to do. Keep them involved and tell them where you would like them to stand

while you work-in the horse. Remember to show the examiner that you realise you are responsible for the pupil's safety both when they are mounted on the horse and when they are unmounted.

3. Take care to check the tack before you begin, and make any necesssary adjustments. Do ask if you need any tack changed or if something is missing. For example, you may require a neck strap and find that one has not been provided.

4. Although the horse will have been worked-in for you, you still need to lunge it for a few moments before you ask the rider to mount. This is to make sure you have some rapport with the horse, and to see if it is working in a calm and active manner. This also gives you a chance to see that the side reins are adjusted to a suitable length.

Content

1. Having spent just a minute or two on working-in, you should be ready for your pupil to mount the horse. They can be involved in helping you to adjust girth, stirrups, side reins, and so on, before mounting.

2. When you are ready to begin make sure the rider is clear on what you would like them to do. Generally, you will ask them to relax, allow you to give the aids, and let you see them in walk and trot so you can assess their usual way of riding and also look to see what needs to be improved.

3. Take care to make sure that the rider keeps a slightly loose rein contact when you have them holding the reins. Many horses will resist and panic if they have both contacts from the side reins and the rider's reins. If you do not know the horse you should not take this risk.

4. At this level it is more important to work on sitting to the trot rather than rising. Although you may like to see a little work in trot rising as part of your general assessment, remember one of the main aims is to improve suppleness and depth of seat.

5. Having assessed the rider on one rein, make a change of rein and take this opportunity to let the rider "quit and cross" their stirrups and tie a knot in their reins. Remember, the rider should always keep a finger through the buckle end of the reins to prevent them from slipping forward down the horse's neck.

6. Explain to the rider what you have seen and where you feel improvements can be made. Make sure you have some positive comments also, so the rider feels positive about their riding.
7. The main body of the lesson will now consist of working on the points already covered. This is where your experience will show. If you have a good eye for assessing the main problem areas in need of improvement, you should be able to give a constructive and helpful lesson. Look for balance, a correct position, freedom from tension, suppleness, and depth of seat. Make sure the rider is sitting straight. You should continue to explain why you are asking them to make various adjustments and how it will help them.
8. You may find one or two physical exercises are helpful, but it is not always necessary to use these to correct the rider.

Conclusion

1. Try to finish the lesson on a high note with the rider feeling the improvement. The rider should have their reins and stirrups back again, and be able to show that they can maintain at least some of the corrections you have made.
2. Finally, ask the rider if he or she has any questions and thank them for being a "guinea pig" rider for you.

Common teacher faults and problems

1. When initially working-in the horse, candidates often fail to ensure that the horse is working actively and listening to their commands. As a result, when they begin to lunge the horse and rider together, the horse's responses to their commands are poor. This makes it difficult for the candidate to give a good lesson.
2. Those candidates who have not gained enough experience in assessing riders on the lunge, may fall into the trap of going through various exercises that seem to bear no relation to that particular rider's problems. It is then quite likely that no rider improvement will be shown.
3. It is quite common in examinations for candidates to ask riders to make

various corrections without giving them any explanation as to why. This usually means there is little rapport between the rider and the teacher, and the rider is less likely to show improvement.

4. If the candidate fails to lunge the horse effectively, it makes it difficult for the rider to feel good paces and establish a good deep seat. Few riders can sit well if the horse is moving in a jerky manner, either rushing or being lazy.

Helpful hints on exam technique

1. When the horse is standing still and you are talking to the rider, remember to position yourself near to the examiner. They can hear your explanations, introduction and conclusion, along with any other comments you have to make.

2. You will probably be sharing an arena with another candidate giving a lunge lesson. Show your awareness for safety and keep an eye on the other horse and anything else going on in the arena. If the other horse gets excitable you may need to bring your horse forward to halt to be safe, as is the case if anyone requests permission to enter or leave the arena.

5   The Lecture

Intermediate teachers need to be competent lecturers. The following is general information on lecturing. Teachers should practise giving different lectures to a variety of students in order to build confidence. You should find it fairly easy to give the 5 minute "lecturette" required in the exam.

In general

Stable/business management subjects and equitation theory are taught to students through lectures which can take many different forms.

a. Lectures can take the form of a theory session in the classroom. A blackboard/whiteboard, flip chart, OHP, and general discussion may be used.

b. Practical instruction in the stable yard can be given. Stable equipment and horses may be used for demonstrations, along with practical participation.

c. Informative videos may be used.

d. Practical tasks or written papers may be set for students to help teachers assess understanding and progress.

Preparation

Good preparation is the key to a successful lecture. If you are poorly prepared you will not instil confidence in the students, and their attention will wander at an early stage. Make sure you have to hand all the information you require. Prepare the lecture area, making sure any props, charts, OHP, blackboard and handouts are ready for use.

Aims and objectives

Students will be more attentive if they understand why they need to know about each subject. A good introduction will explain the purpose of your talk/demonstration, as well as the subject matter you intend to cover. For example, if you were giving a lecture on feeding, your aims may include:

1. Teach recognition of a variety of feed stuffs; to know whether they are of good or poor quality, and how to prepare them.
2. Teach the rules of, and a variety of systems for, feeding and watering.
3. Teach suitable quantities of feed for horses of various sizes in a variety of work.

Your objectives may include:

1. Enable students to select suitable types and quantities of feed for a variety of horses in their care.
2. Enable students to select suitable systems of feeding and watering for horses in their care.

Timing

The amount of time available will dictate how much of each subject you can cover per session. It may help some teachers to make a time plan to help you keep to the subject and not allow yourself to be sidetracked. Some subjects will need to be broken down into small sections. This allows for breaks, which may be quite short, for coffee, questions, etc., or may form a good cut-off point for that day. The lecture could then be resumed at a suitable time, for example the next day.

Time plans can help you to be flexible without losing sight of your goal. There are many occasions when students' questions or their ability to grasp a subject, may lead you off on a tangent. It is important to answer these questions and to check the students' understanding, but having done this you can then return to your original plan, knowing how much extra time you need to allow to complete that subject.

Resources

Resources include anything that will aid the delivery of the lecture. Your choice of resources will obviously be governed by what is available to you but will also depend upon the size of the group you are teaching, and their level of experience and their age group. When making your choice, you should bear in mind that you are more likely to keep the attention of the students, and make a lasting impression with your lecture, if you aim to stimulate as many of the five senses as possible. With a little thought, many horse-related subjects can incorporate hearing, seeing, touching, smelling, and sometimes tasting. Too many lectures rely on hearing alone, with groups of students listening to the lecturer for long periods. This often leads to loss of concentration due to a lack of stimuli.

Locations

Where possible, prepare and choose your location carefully; it will make a tremendous difference to the students' ability to concentrate. Students will be uncomfortable and may fidget or even fall asleep if the room is either too cold or too hot. The same problem will result from inappropriate seating and tables. Constant interruptions, perhaps from people coming into the room, from noises or from activity outside the window, distract everyone, including the teacher. Although many stable yards have limited facilities, try to select quiet and comfortable surroundings.

Lectures and demonstrations that take place in a stable yard must be planned with regard to safety, weather conditions and visibility. Crowding a group of students into a small stable with a horse is potentially dangerous, as the horse may kick out or swing round. Even if the horse behaves well, it is still unlikely that everyone will have a good view. However, if just one or two students are attending the lecture, the stable could be a suitable environment, providing the horse is tied up and everyone keeps to the same side of the horse at the same time.

Ideally, stable yard lectures should take place with the horse tied up outside, leaving enough room for the students to stand or sit around in a large semi-circle. They should be well away from the horse so that there is no danger of kicks or any injuries. This will also give the lecturer room to move safely around the horse. If weather conditions are poor, this area needs to be under cover and well lit. All yard areas should be enclosed so that if the horse gets loose there will be gates and fences blocking all its exits.

Voice

Providing you know your subject well and have made a good plan, you should have no difficulty in knowing what to say. However, it is the way it is said that makes all the difference. Students need a clear and interesting voice to listen to. If you speak too slowly or too fast, with too many "umms" or "Okays" you will not hold the students' attention. It can be helpful to make a tape recording of one of your lectures and listen to yourself. Each individual will have different problems to overcome. Think of pausing instead of saying "umm", vary the tone of your voice and try to speak with enthusiasm.

Reading directly from your notes will not work as you will be looking down all the time, unable to see the students' reactions. In this situation, the students might as well read a book on their own. Notes should be used to remind you of each point you intend to cover but the main content should be in your head. For this reason, you must know your subject thoroughly.

Visual aids

The visual aid is very powerful and should help most people to understand and retain information. Your choice of what to use and when will affect the quality of the lecture.

1. Handouts. A clear photocopy for the student to keep and refer back to will eliminate the need for hasty sketches during the lecture or inaccurate drawings made from memory. It is better to issue handouts at the

end of a lecture, having already told the students that they will be available, otherwise they become a distraction, drawing attention away from the speaker.

2. Overhead projector (OHP). Providing you use this simple piece of equipment well, it will help you to convey information. You must set up the OHP in advance. Project a drawing on to the screen, then stand at the back of the room and make sure it is clearly visible. The whole procedure becomes an annoying distraction if the picture/printing is too small or blurred to be understood. Check that you are also expert at putting the acetate in the right way up. Although you have prepared handouts for the end of the lecture, you will probably need to draw the students' attention to particular items during the lecture. For example, if you are giving a lecture on "Shoeing", you may not have examples of all the tools available. If you draw and display them individually on the OHP the students' attention will be focused on each item as you choose to show it. The OHP enlarges pictures, which is particularly advantageous when working with large groups of students. You can also build up pictures by laying one acetate on top of another. Making up the acetates in advance facilitates the flow of your lecture and saves time. The acetates can be kept and used over and over again.

3. Pictures/Photographs. When a particular item is not available to you, a picture of that item is the next best thing. If you are not a good illustrator it can be helpful to compile a folder of useful pictures; for example, different breeds or colours of horses, poisonous plants, items of tack, and so on. Taking photographs can be a helpful way of adding to your collection. The time taken to pass a picture around a large group will interrupt the flow of your lecture; therefore, pictures are most useful for small groups who can gather around and look at the picture together, unless the picture is large enough to display in front of the group, or a slide that can be projected on to a screen.

4. Video. Combining both sight and sound, the video is an excellent way of putting information across. Always watch the video yourself first, to check its content and quality, before showing it to the students.

5. Blackboard and chalk or whiteboard and pens. These are useful for those quick illustrations that help you to explain a particular point to a

particular group, providing you are a confident illustrator and can spell properly. Most classroom lectures can be helped along with the use of a board to write on, but used on its own "chalk and talk" is not a very stimulating way of presenting most lectures.

6. Flipchart. A useful aid that can be set up more easily than the OHP headings and illustrations can be drawn in advance and re-used many times.

7. Demonstrations. This is probably the most useful form of visual instruction for stable management and the only real three-dimensional way of showing students how a job is done.

8. Props. Combining seeing and touching makes a lecture more interesting and easier to understand. For example, being able to handle the shoeing tools or a clipping machine, is far more effective than just looking at pictures. Props also help you to employ the senses of smell or even taste. Aromas can be powerful memory jerkers and can help focus the students' attention. This can be helpful when learning about feed stuffs and veterinary applications.

In order to make sure that the information you give has been absorbed and understood, you will need to obtain feedback from the students. While watching students carry out various tasks, and by asking them questions, you will soon discover whether or not they have understood and remembered everything they have been taught. You can also gain feedback during each lecture by listening to questions asked, and by looking at students' reactions.

The students also need feedback from the lecturer. They need to know if they are interpreting instructions and answering questions correctly. They need to know, too, if the standard of their work is acceptable. So feedback is very important in both directions. By using different lecturing techniques you will accommodate the needs of a range of students who learn and absorb information in various ways.

However, you should be careful not to let the use of resources become more important than the content of the lecture. It is possible to use too many visual aids and demonstrations, which can result in confusion. For this reason, most lectures should consist of a balanced combination of theory, demonstrations and/or active participation, along with a carefully selected variety of resources.

The "Lecturette" exam format

The lecturette is to be just 5 minutes long. Each candidate is given a lecture subject when they arrive at the beginning of the examination day. You then have at least half an hour or so to prepare your subject. You can use any books or notes you have brought with you, and can take notes to work from into the exam.

You are to imagine that you are lecturing to students preparing for the Stage III/Preliminary Teaching Test. Therefore the subjects given may include anything that students are required to know about for that level, and anything you may need to teach them if they were working for you at an equestrian establishment. The following are a few examples of possible subjects.

a. Stable construction – what you like and dislike.
b. Explain to a new working pupil the daily routine and timetable in your yard.
c. Instructions to staff on receiving a livery.
d. Maintenance of an indoor school.
e. Safety measures in and around the yard.
f. The reception and care of riding clients.

The chief examiner will decide, on the day, what subjects to give. Although the time allowed is very short, it is possible to put across a considerable amount of information in 5 minutes. You should aim to show that you can structure the lecture well, make a good plan, present yourself confidently, speak clearly, deliver the lecture at a good pace, and give sound and relevant information. You will be provided with a board to write on which can be helpful in the presentation of your lecture.

Introduction
Begin with the usual opening of "Good morning/afternoon, my name

is," then follow on with the title of the lecture and your aims and objectives.

Content

It is important to show that you can put over information clearly and logically. If the examiner's impression is of a muddled and confusing lecture they will not feel that you could teach students to the required level. Break down the subject matter into logical sections. If your subject is concise in nature include plenty of detail, but if the subject is big highlight the main points. Try to keep to 5 minutes, you will only be asked to stop if you go on for too long.

Conclusion

Remember the objectives you started out with and use these to help with the conclusion. For example, one of the objectives for the lecture on feeding was to enable students to select suitable types and quantities of feed for a variety of horses in their care. In conclusion you may say, "If you follow the rules and information I have outlined you should be able to select suitable types and quantities of feed for the horses you care for." A final sentence of, "That concludes my lecture. Thank you." makes a neat finish.

Common teacher faults and problems

1. Some candidates write too much on their notes and end up reading from them. As mentioned above, this does not demonstrate an ability to give a lecture. Also, if the candidate loses their place they can then be completely thrown, and unable to continue.
2. Although the examiner will allow for nerves at this level each candidate should be very experienced at standing up in front of a group and talking. Some candidates give the impression that they are very inexperienced when they deliver a muddled mix of information with constant "umms" and "ers".
3. Some candidates that choose to use the blackboard are quite poor at writing clearly and straight. It is not good enough to say, "Excuse my poor writing and spelling", this does nothing to instil confidence in a

group of pupils. Make sure you have had sufficient practice before the exam day

4. Conclusions are often poor or non-existent. Some candidates just say, "That's it." This is unprofessional and not what an examiner is looking for in an Intermediate teacher. Make sure you have a good conclusion.

Helpful hints on exam technique

1. Practise giving some 5 minute lectures at home. You may be a very experienced lecturer but more familiar with giving lectures of 1 hour in length. It is a little different when it is only 5 minutes.

2. Although usual lecturing practice would involve talking to your pupils and looking for feedback, don't expect this in your exam. You will be lecturing to your fellow candidates and they will have other things on their minds.

3. Make sure anything you write on the blackboard is concise. As you only have 5 minutes, writing long sentences does not help your examiner to assess your lecturing technique.

6 Teaching and Equitation Theory

In general

In both the Intermediate Teaching Test and the Stage IV exam, candidates will discuss teaching and training techniques with an examiner. This will be a group discussion lasting for approximately one hour. Questions will be asked on lesson content, lungeing on the flat and over fences, preparing horse and rider for competitions up to Elementary dressage, Newcomers Show Jumping and BHS Novice Horse Trials level. For the Intermediate Teaching Test the questions relate more to teaching horse and rider while for the Stage IV exam the questions relate more to training the horse from early handling onwards.

Rules and regulations

It is important to be familiar with the current rules governing each discipline. As a teacher and rider you need to know, for example, how old a horse must be to compete in affiliated competitions, what tack is permissible, whether a dressage test will be ridden in a 20mx40m arena or a 20mx60m arena, what clothing and equipment the rider may use, and so on. The rules change from time to time so the current rule book for the year should be consulted. The following is a summary of some of the rules you are most likely to need to keep up to date with.

Dressage
Equipment for the rider
a. It is compulsory for anyone mounted on a horse at an affiliated dres-

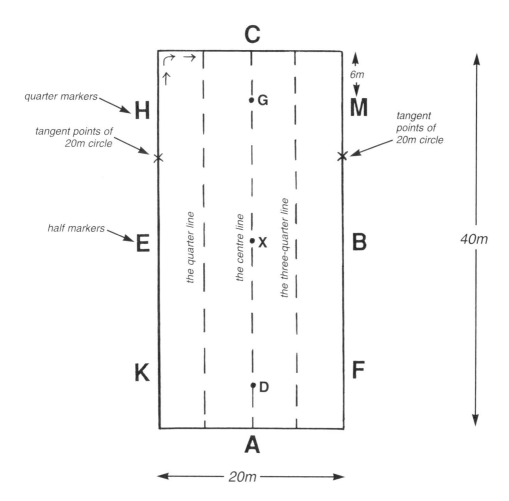

Dimensions and markers for a riding arena, 20mx40m. D and G are points on the centre line level with the quarter markers.

sage competition to wear a hard hat. Check the rule book for the most up to date hat standard required.

b. Gloves must be worn.

c. Whips of any length may be carried in either hand.

Plan of 20mx60m arena. (Note dimensions.)

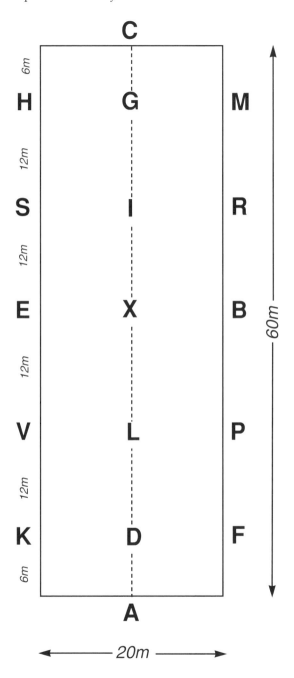

Equipment for the horse

a. No brightly-coloured or Western style saddles are permitted, and no saddle covers of any sort.

b. An ordinary snaffle bridle should be worn for Preliminary and Novice level competitions. From Elementary to Advanced Medium an ordinary snaffle or double bridle can be worn. At Advanced level a double bridle is worn.

c. Only the bits illustrated are permitted. No bit guards are permitted.

d. A noseband must be worn. A drop, flash, or cavesson noseband may be worn with a snaffle bridle. A cavesson noseband only, may be worn with a double bridle. Grakle nosebands may only be worn for horse trials dressage.

e. Breatsplates are permitted, but martingales, side reins, running reins, and so on are not.

f. Boots and bandages are not permitted. Many riders use bandages or boots when working in, which is permissible, but you must remember to remove them before entering the dressage arena otherwise you will be eliminated.

Horse trials
For the dressage section

The same permitted and not permitted tack as for pure dressage with the exception of the grakle noseband, which is permitted, and whips which riders are not allowed to carry in any test.

Showjumping and cross-country

a. Running and Irish martingales are permitted, but standing martingales are not.

b. Gags and hackamores may be used.

c. Riders must wear a body protector and crash hat for the cross-country phase. The current rule book will state the required standard for both of these.

BSJA Showjumping
For the rider

a. A hard hat with a retaining harness that attaches to the hat at more

Permitted bits

1 and **2**
*Ordinary
snaffle with
double-jointed
mouthpiece.*

3
*Ordinary
snaffle with
single-jointed
mouthpiece.*

4
*Racing or "D"-
ring snaffle.*

5
*Egg-butt
snaffle.*

6
*Egg-butt
snaffle with
cheeks.*

7
Fulmer snaffle.

8
*Snaffle with
upper cheeks
only.*

9
*Rubber
snaffle.*

10
*Unjointed
snaffle.*

11
*Hanging cheek
snaffle.*

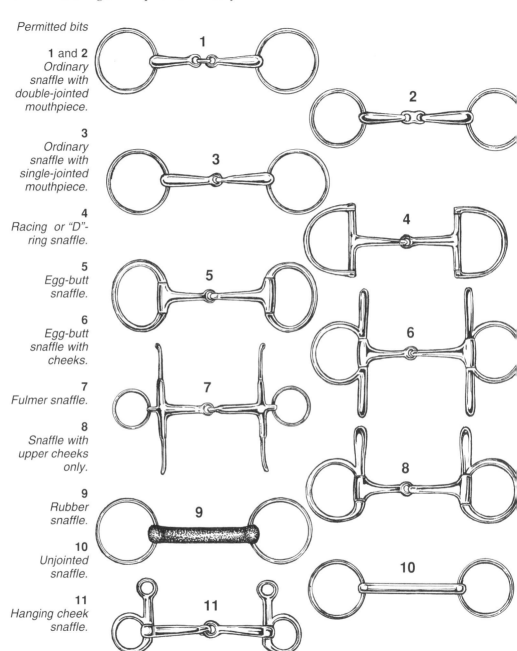

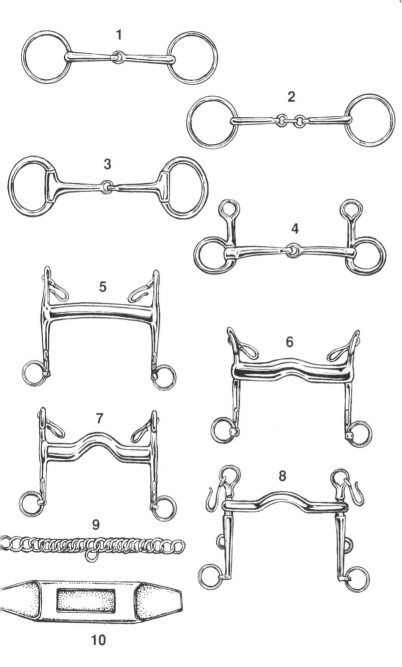

Permitted bits

1 *Ordinary bradoon bit.*

2 *Bradoon bit with two joints*

3 *Egg-butt bradoon bit.*

4 *Hanging cheek bradoon.*

5 *Half-moon curb bit.*

6 *Curb bit with curved cheeks and tongue groove.*

7 *Curb bit with tongue groove.*

8 *Curb bit with tongue groove and sliding mouthpiece.*

9 *Curb chain.*

10 *Rubber cover for curb chain.*

than two points must be worn. The harness must be done up. See the current rule book for the recommended hat standard.

b. Jackets must be worn along with shirt and white tie or stock.
   For the horse
a. Standing and running martingales may be used.
b. Market Harboroughs may be used but only with a plain snaffle.
e. Gags and hackamores are permitted.

Grading systems
Dressage

In pure dressage, horses are graded using a points system. If they achieve a mark for their test of 60–61.99 per cent they are awarded 1 point. From there each extra percentage equals another point up to 67 per cent or over for which 7 points are awarded. A horse with up to 37 points is Preliminary level; up to 74 points Novice level; and up to 124 points Elementary level.

Horse trials

A points system is also used for horse trials. Horses with less than 21 points are Grade 3, from 21–60 points they are Grade 2, and with 61 or more points they are Grade 1. Points are awarded according to the final placings, with 6 points for the first place, going down to 1 point for sixth place according to the number of starters. Pre-Novice horse trials are restricted to Grade 3 horses without points.

BSJA Showjumping

The BSJA office keeps a grading record for each horse based on the amount of prize money won. Horses start as Grade C which is for nil to £799. Grade B is for £800 to £1,799, and Grade A is £1,800 and over.

Paces and movements

You may be asked to explain various school figures and transitions – as well as terms like balance, on the forehand, rhythm and tempo, outline, above the bit, hollow, and so on – and describe the qualities you are looking for in the various paces. All of these are outlined in Chapter 2, The

Dressage Lesson. You should feel that you can explain and discuss any of the content of this chapter.

Jumping

Questions will also be asked on different aspects of jumping: How would you improve the balance of horse and rider? When would you use trotting poles? What types of cross-country fences may cause you particular problems?, and so on. All of these aspects are outlined in Chapter 3, The Jumping Lesson. You should feel that you can explain and discuss any of the content of this chapter.

Lungeing

Questions will be asked on lungeing the horse, the rider, and lungeing over poles or jumps. You should feel able to discuss any of the content of Chapter 4, The Lunge Lesson.

Examinations

As an Intermediate teacher you would be expected to be able to train riders up to Stage III standard. You may be asked questions relating to the qualities you are looking for in a rider of this level. Make sure you have not forgotten the requirements of the stages examinations.

For example, at Stage III:

a. The rider should demonstrate that they are effective and sympathetic in their riding. They should be able to maintain a supple, balanced, and correct seat in all paces on schooled horses, and when jumping.

b. They should be capable of jumping various schooled horses over show jumps up to 1m and cross-country fences up to 0.91m.

c. When riding on the flat and over fences they should be able to apply the aids smoothly and, when asked, show that they have a clear understanding of why these aids are used.

d. They must be able to demonstrate their ability to ride using both a snaffle and a double bridle.

e. When questioned, they should give answers that show they were able to correctly feel whether the horses they rode had good paces, whether they performed movements correctly and whether they responded well to their aids.

Helpful hints on exam technique
1. Make sure you have practised answering questions on all of the above subjects. You may think you know the theory, but giving informative answers to questions needs practice. For example, if you were asked what is meant by the term "above the bit" could you give a clear and concise answer?
2. Remember, there will be different opinions on various subjects. If your opinion is different from that expressed by one of your fellow candidates it is better not to say that you think they are wrong; simply state what you feel about the subject under discussion. You may both be correct, but it is always unnerving for the other person if you say that they are wrong.

7 Business and Yard Management

In general

In the Intermediate Teaching Test candidates will discuss various aspects of business and yard management. This will be a group discussion lasting approximately 50 minutes.

The office

A number of books and records will need to be kept to ensure the smooth running of any business, along with various different filing systems which can be used to help all staff locate the information they need.

Filing systems

a. Keeping information in files in alphabetical order of horses' names, or clients' names, or names of staff, is the most basic way of keeping information easily accessible to all who need it.
b. When there is a lot of information to file, then filing cabinets and files will be needed. If there is only a small amount of information, such as a person's name and address, then a card index using alphabetical order, can be more convenient.
c. Date order may be more useful for some information. For example, keeping a note of when the vet or farrier called and what work was undertaken at that time. In this case a diary may be all that is needed.

d. Larger businesses may have a computer system and keep all their information on computer files.

e. Often, information needs to be kept in more than one place. For example, the vet's visit may be recorded in a diary with the work undertaken, and each horse attended may also have a note in its file of what was done and when.

f. Wall charts are another way of recording information and planning ahead at the same time.

g. To choose the system or systems that you prefer, you need to consider financial constraints, the size of the business, and what type of system suits you. Some people work well with a diary, while others forget to look in the diary or record events. Others prefer a wall chart because it is easy to look at each day if displayed in a prominent place.

h. Whatever system you choose, remember to consider leaving room for expansion. It is likely to be tedious and time consuming if a system needs to be completely re-thought to make room for recording more information.

Equipment

a. Financial constraints and the size of the business will dictate the type and extent of the equipment found in each office.

b. A telephone will be essential. This may be a payphone so that incoming calls can be received but outgoing calls can be kept under control if the office also doubles up as a rest room and coffee area. A mobile phone may be used if the person in charge is instructor, yard worker and secretary all rolled into one. At the other end of the scale, larger establishments may have an internal telephone system, switchboard and fax machine to cope with all their incoming and outgoing calls.

c. Computers are commonplace now in most medium to large offices, as they can be used to file information which can easily be added to, as well as making the accounts easier to keep under control. They may be beyond the needs and scope of the smaller business, however.

d. Basic office furniture like chairs, desks, drawers, and filing cabinets are always needed.

e. Diaries, loose-leaf files, card indexes, headed notepaper, envelopes, and other books in which information can be recorded are all needed for efficient recording of information, communication, and therefore smooth running of the business.

f. A photocopier is always very useful, but an expensive item for a very small business. They do vary from very small desktop models to state of the art colour copiers with many additional functions.

g. Anything from a lockable box to a cash register will be needed for the safe keeping of money. A petty cash box will also be needed.

Books and records

a. All horses and ponies kept at the premises should have their details recorded and kept in a filing system. The information should include the horse's age, height, breeding, current work programme, current feeding programme, vaccination status, blemishes, vices, freeze mark or brand. It should also include a description of each horse – or, better still, photographs, showing the horse from each side and in winter and summer coat. Records of this sort, along with any registration papers with proof of ownership, are invaluable if a horse is stolen.

b. A veterinary book should be kept detailing vet visits and the work done. This book along with the horse's individual file should carry details of any problems peculiar to a particular horse. For example, if a horse is allergic to penicillin it must be clearly noted where everyone will be aware of this.

c. A record is needed of when each horse's vaccinations are due. A wall chart may be useful for this.

d. A shoeing book should be kept to record the work done and it will help with the planning of when the next visit from the farrier should be and the horses that will need attention.

e. A system for recording additional services supplied to livery horses will be needed in order to keep track of charges to be made. For example, when a horse is clipped or schooled it should be recorded then transferred to the livery bill at the end of the month.

f. Records of each client, bookings made, financial records, staff, insurance, and health and safety requirements must also be kept in a well organised office, as detailed below.

Grading and booking clients

a. When a new client first makes contact with the riding school their details should immediately be recorded for future reference. In some schools this may mean filling in a card, in others files may be kept for each client, or details may be put into the computer. Details should include name, address, telephone number, age, height, weight, and riding ability.

b. Whatever the client's riding standard, they should be given an assessment lesson before being advised on suitable groups they can join, riding courses they may like to enrol on, or the best time of day for private lessons. During the assessment lesson the instructor will be able to assess the rider's abilities and therefore be able to put them into a grade relevant to that particular riding school.

c. Each riding school should have a grading system that will help them to keep riders of a similar standard together, and make it easier to choose suitable horses and instructors for each rider. A grading system may be unique to that particular school, or the school may choose to use a ready-made system like the Progressive Riding Tests set out by the BHS.

d. Having assessed the new client, every effort should be made to encourage them to become regular riders at the school. This is often done by offering a block booking at a reduced rate. Some schools make offers such as pay for five lessons in advance and each one is reduced, or pay for six lessons in advance and receive the seventh lesson free of charge, and so on.

e. Payment for several lessons in advance also helps with the problem of cancellation fees. Once the money has been taken, 50 per cent of the fee can be retained in the case of a cancellation, or 100 per cent if the cancellation is made at the last minute. Most schools have a policy of asking for a minimum of 24 hours' notice, and will transfer the booking to a future date or different time if an agreed amount of notice is given.

f. It is also advisable to arrange for your clients to book and pay for their next lesson a week in advance to avoid the problem of a last-minute cancellation of a lesson that has not been paid for. It is best to operate a policy of payment at time of booking. Explain, to those clients who fail to pay at the time of booking that their lesson cannot be confirmed until payment is received.

g. It is important to have a nominated person available to take bookings and payment at the appropriate times throughout the day if the systems in place are going to work smoothly.

h. The number of clients attending the riding school, and the number of teaching staff available, will dictate how many group lessons or private lessons take place each day. A pattern will soon emerge that shows when the most popular times are for group lessons for adults, children, the more advanced, and beginners. New clients can then be encouraged to attend at the appropriate times. This will help with forward planning, allocation of horses, and allocation of staff teaching hours. Private lessons can be fitted in around these groups depending on the availability of staff, horses and teaching areas.

i. When planning these regular group rides the following questions must be considered: How many horses are available? Are the horses of suitable type and size? Have the horses had sufficient rest time since their last working session? Have the horses worked their full quota of hours that day? Is there an instructor available capable of teaching the group in question? Is there a teaching area suitable for the type of lesson to be given?

j. When allocating the hours that horses can work the following should be considered: beginner level lessons will not be very taxing for the horse, so it may be able to do several lessons of this type. Advanced level lessons, particularly private lessons, will be hard work for the horse and it should not be expected to do more than two or three lessons in one day. The horse's hours should be spread evenly through the day so it has sufficient rest and recovery time. Some horses may be fitter than others and able to do more work. Older or very young horses should not be given as much work. Working sessions should consist of a variety of dressage, jumping, and hacking in order not to over-tax the horse in any one area. Fit horses can usually work for around 4 hours per day with one day off per week.

Accounts

a. Whether you run the smallest or the largest of businesses you must keep a record of all expenditure and income in order to give your accountant the necessary information. Your accountant will then be able to make sure that your VAT and income tax payments are made as required by law. Each area of your business needs a detailed record book.

b. If you have liveries, the details of bills going out must be recorded along with payments made. The system should show what each person has been billed for and whether or not any payments are outstanding.

c. If you buy and sell horses, records of your purchases along with any bills sent to you or receipts must be kept, as well as copies of any bills sent out by you. Records should show what payments have been made and if any are outstanding.

d. Payments made by your riding clients must be recorded. It will help you to analyse the most successful aspects of your business if you break down the payments to show income from children's lessons, income from adult's lessons, income from holiday courses and so on.

f. If sales exceed a specific threshold figure a business must register for VAT. Once registered, the business must charge VAT on all relevant sales. The VAT collected must be paid over to the Customs and Excise on a regular basis. All records kept must detail VAT paid or charged.

g. It is the employer's responsibility to collect income tax due from any staff employed. The PAYE (Pay As You Earn) system must be used. The employer is also responsible for making sure that National Insurance contributions are paid both for themselves and their employees. Obviously, records must be kept.

h. Records of all the business assets must be kept. For example, vehicles, horses, buildings, and fixtures.

i. All of the above will be needed by your accountant for preparation of the year-end accounts.

Insurance

a. Some insurance is required by law and some is advisable. It will be up to the individual to decide what insurance to take out beyond that which is required by law.

b. Public liability insurance is required by law if your establishment is open to the public and is for the protection of the public while they are on your premises if an accident occurs that is due to your negligence.

c. Employers' liability insurance is required by law if you employ staff. It covers accident and injury to staff that may occur due to your negligence while they were working for you. This insurance certificate must be displayed in a place where all staff can see it. If you are employed yourself, you should make sure there is an employer's liability insurance certificate displayed for you to see.

d. All vehicles to be used on the road must have third party, fire and theft insurance. It may be advisable to have fully comprehensive insurance if the vehicle is fairly new and likely to be expensive to replace if stolen or written off in an accident.

e. Any other insurance can be taken out if you decide it is the safest way to proceed. You should make sure your livery owners insure their own horses and tack. You may like to take out a policy to cover you for your liability to the horses in your care. As their keeper, not necessarily their owner, you are liable, for example, if the horses in your care escape and cause damage. You could insure large quantities of hay and straw, buildings, and your own horses and tack.

f. If you are a member of the BHS you will automatically have free personal liability insurance and equestrian-related insurance. This could prove extremely useful if, for example, you were found to have caused an accident while out hacking. It would be wise to encourage any livery owners, or staff, to become BHS members for this reason alone.

Health and safety

a. It is the employer's duty to ensure the health and safety of their employees as far as is reasonably practicable. They must make sure that machinery and substances used are safe and that the workplace and environment are safe. Employers should also provide instruction and training in how to carry out work safely. The Health and Safety Executive (HSE) publish booklets which detail the requirements of the law.

b. Employers with five or more employees must have a written health and safety policy statement which all their employees should be familiar with. This statement should set out the employer's arrangements and organisation for health and safety.

c. The Reporting of Injuries, Diseases and Dangerous Occurrences Regulations 1985 (RIDDOR) requires employers to report certain injuries and accidents. Reports are made to the local environmental health department. There are set forms which have to be filled in if someone dies or suffers certain serious injuries as a result of an accident in connection with their work. Dangerous occurrences must also be reported.

d. An accident book must be kept and all accidents should be recorded noting the person's name, date and time of accident, what happened and where, and what action was taken. This information is necessary for several reasons: by keeping a record it may be possible to see that a certain person is frequently involved in accidents and may be in need of more training. A picture may emerge showing a particular horse causing accidents. In this case the horse may need schooling or need its work programme changed. The accident book must be available for staff and clients to look at; if clear records are kept both staff and clients should be reassured that the management are aware of accidents occurring. If any questions are asked for legal reasons, as in the case of an insurance claim, the accident details will be readily available.

e. There should always be at least one appointed person in charge of first aid. They should preferably have first-aid training. There are health and safety regulations covering the workplace which vary according to the nature of the work and hazards involved.

f. The Control of Substances Hazardous to Health (COSHH) Regulations require employers to assess and control exposure of their staff to hazardous substances. In equestrian establishments hazardous substances may include dust, veterinary products, disinfectants, and diseases such as tetanus and leptospirosis. The employer should assess the risks, take measures to minimise and control the risks and give staff training in how to work with these risks.

g. The HSE booklets available give detailed information on each of the above. Employers should obtain copies of these booklets and make sure that they themselves are complying with all the necessary regulations.

h. Remember, all the basic stable management instruction given to trainees is relevant health and safety training. This includes: teaching safe lifting and carrying techniques; teaching how to inspect tack for worn leather, stitching in need of repair, and any other signs that it may be unsafe; teaching which protective clothing should be worn for stable work, clipping, handling horses and riding; teaching good stable management practices so that equipment is handled safely and put away, and yard areas are kept tidy to prevent accidents and minimise the spread of fire should it break out; teaching about stable construction and maintenance checks that should be made to keep the working environment safe; and so on.

i. Fire extinguishers and other fire-fighting equipment such as hoses, water troughs, and buckets of sand, should be regularly maintained. All staff and students should be familiar with the fire drill.

j. Training staff and students for, and encouraging them to take, the Riding and Road Safety examination is another important part of health and safety training.

Security

a. Theft of horses and of tack is all too common. If you decide to take out insurance against this happening, you are quite likely to receive a discount from your insurance company if your horses are freeze marked and your tack is security marked.

b. When a horse is freeze marked, the freeze marking company send a representative to your premises to brand your horse with irons cooled in liquid nitrogen. This is a painless process which in time leaves a white hair mark on a horse with a dark coat or a bald mark on a grey or cream coloured horse. The mark takes a few weeks to come through and is usually a combination of letters and figures which is entered into a register. If the horse is stolen its registered freeze mark number can quickly be circulated to police stations and horse sales around the country and therefore aid speedy recovery and return to its owner.

c. There are various different ways of marking tack for security purposes. In general, using a post code is most common. This can be stamped into the leather work of any item of tack and will help police to return stolen items to their owners.

d. If your tack and horses are marked in this way it is a good idea to prominently display signs that tell any prospective thieves that this is the case. This may help to deter them in the first place as they know it will be difficult to sell a freeze-marked horse or security-marked tack.

e. Tackrooms should also be made secure with the use of alarms, strong doors and locks, and preferably no windows so the tack is not easily located.

f. It is always more difficult to secure horses as fences can be cut and doors unbolted. However, you can make a thief's job more difficult by using strong gates and padlocks to secure fields and all yard areas. Make sure gates cannot be lifted off their hinges. Use night lighting around the yard, and where possible have someone living on site.

Staff

a. Employing staff can be one of the most expensive aspects of a business. However, staff can be one of your greatest assets if they are well trained and well treated.

b. If you employ working pupils who work in return for their tuition and a small wage, you must remember that they will require a fair amount of your attention and teaching time. You could end up spending more time teaching working pupils than you spend on teaching paying clients. As working pupils come to you to learn and hopefully achieve certain qualifications, they will be inexperienced and probably not very fit for this type of work to begin with. You should not expect them to look after as many horses as an experienced paid groom. They may be able to look after two stabled horses and maybe one or two field-kept ponies.

c. A paid groom, of course, will cost you more to employ but will leave you more time for teaching, planning and organising, so you may be more well off in the long run. An experienced groom, with no other responsibilities, could look after four stabled horses and one or two grass-kept ponies.

d. In an expanding business you may need a yard manager or at least an assistant manager. Their job would be to oversee the smooth running of the daily routine, making sure that grooms and working pupils carry out their tasks correctly and to the required standard, giving them help and guidance where necessary and reporting back to you with any problems.

e. You may need qualified teaching staff to help you if you have a busy yard and more clients requiring lessons than you can cope with on your own.

f. If you have clients who want to hack out, you may be able to let your staff do this while you teach lessons in the school. Anyone escorting a hack should definitely be qualified in some way. If they do not have teaching qualifications, then they may be able to take the Riding Escort's Certificate. Accidents can happen so easily when out hacking. The escorts must be trained in how to escort a hack safely and what to do in the event of an accident. If they have qualifications to prove that they have received this training this will be to your advantage should there be any complaints or legal action following an accident, as well as being reassuring for both you and the clients.

g. Hacking out usually involves some riding on the roads which can be a very hazardous business these days. For this reason it is a good idea to encourage all your clients to take the Riding and Road Safety Test.

How the BHS can help

a. The BHS runs a riding schools approval scheme. Riding schools are approved at different levels according to their facilities and what they are able to offer.

b. A riding school that would like BHS approval applies to the BHS. An inspector will visit the school and see if the standard of care for the horses, the condition of the equipment, the working conditions and standard of teaching are all of the required standard for approval. If they are, the riding school will become BHS approved on payment of the annual fee. The school will be put on the BHS list of approved schools and appear in the BHS *Where to Ride* booklet.

c. The riding school will be entitled to display a plaque which states that it is BHS approved for that year. Prospective clients will be encouraged to know that the school keeps good standards. Also, many people contact the BHS to ask for a list of approved riding schools in their area when they are first looking for a suitable establishment at which to learn.

d. The riding school will be subject to unannounced spot checks from the BHS inspectors, and will be checked up on, again unannounced, if any complaints are received from the public.

e. The insurance benefits of BHS membership have been mentioned above. If you become a member of the BHS you also have access to a free legal helpline – which can be of great assistance to anyone setting up an equestrian business. Other benefits include access to the BHS examination system and you will receive each year three free issues of the BHS magazine and a member's year book. You will also be supporting a very worthwhile charity.

f. The BHS has a register of instructors which is of great value to both pupils and instructors alike. Instructors must have a current first-aid certificate, be BHS qualified and be prepared to abide by a code of conduct. They also have insurance cover. Anyone can obtain a copy of the

BHS register and check up on their instructor's details. Clients will be reassured to know that an instructor's qualifications are genuine, that they have first-aid knowledge in the event of an accident and insurance cover if a claim is brought against them.

Helpful hints on exam technique

1. As with the equitation theory section described earlier, make sure that you have practised answering questions on all the above subjects. Be sure you can put your thoughts and ideas into words.
2. Check your facts before the examination as rules and regulations are constantly being updated.

Index